MILWAUKEE
FOOD

LORI FREDRICH | *Photography by Joe Laedtke*

MILWAUKEE FOOD

A HISTORY OF CREAM CITY CUISINE

Bon Appetit!

[signature]

2015

AMERICAN PALATE

Published by American Palate
A Division of The History Press
Charleston, SC 29403
www.historypress.net

Cover images: Chef Mo of RuYi at Potawatomi Hotel & Casino. *Joe Laedtke*; produce grown by farms in Milwaukee's urban periphery and sold at area farmers' markets. *Joe Laedtke*.

First published 2015

Manufactured in the United States

ISBN 978.1.62619.670.4

Library of Congress Control Number: 2015945703

Notice: The information in this book is true and complete to the best of our knowledge. It is offered without guarantee on the part of the author or The History Press. The author and The History Press disclaim all liability in connection with the use of this book.

Contents

Acknowledgements

I am ever grateful to the many individuals who have supported me as I've pursued my passions for food and writing. This book is largely dedicated to the chefs, entrepreneurs and food producers who opened their kitchens to me over the years, allowing me a firsthand glimpse into their world.

Thank you to the Marcus Corporation—specifically Jacob Ruck and Cassie Scrima—whose efforts in assisting me to capture elements of the history and imagery of Milwaukee's historic hotels were priceless.

I owe a large debt to my husband and muse, Paul, who cooked countless dinners and performed myriad household chores in order to free up my time for writing. He was always there with soothing words of encouragement, and often a glass of bourbon, as I wracked my brain for the strength and courage to finish what sometimes felt like an impossible task—to capture the spirit and passion of a food city on the rise.

To Ellie Martin Cliffe, who swooped in at the last minute to offer her kind services in proofing the manuscript: I am indebted. I'm also grateful to Joe Laedtke, whose photographic efforts—however arduous—resulted in a work that tells stories not only with words but with pictures. And I would be remiss if I didn't acknowledge the support of Bobby Tanzilo, managing editor at OnMilwaukee.com, for seeing my potential and not only encouraging my hire as a full-time writer but also recommending me as a potential author to The History Press.

I owe my final thanks to the team at The History Press, including production editor Ryan Finn for his keen eye and commissioning editor Ben

Gibson, who guided me through the publishing process with deft hands and kindhearted direction.

And lastly, an apology. For many reasons, this work is not exhaustive nor encyclopedic in its scope. A variety of chefs, restaurants and producers—all of whom have influenced Milwaukee's food culture in significant ways—receive no mention in its pages. As with most works of this nature, there are omissions, and I apologize to anyone who is disappointed not to find their favorite eatery within its pages.

Introduction

This book is a love letter of sorts. It's the story of how a bustling blue-collar town—a largely overlooked gem known best for its beer and bratwurst—became a destination for food lovers. It's also the story of many dedicated people—producers, chefs and entrepreneurs—who have contributed to the creation of a unique food culture unlike that of any other American city.

For years, Milwaukee crouched beneath the shadow of Chicago, victim of a widespread inferiority complex that focused largely on its deficits while overlooking the significant assets of being "a big city with a small-town feel." Bogged down by the loss of its historically industrial roots, the city seemed to lack identity. And a sense of displacement ensued, clouding development and creating a self-depreciating narrative that was largely unfounded.

Many thanks are owed to visionaries like Chef Sanford D'Amato and Joe and Paul Bartolotta, who saw a future in the Cream City, laying down their culinary roots and assisting in a sea change for the city's food scene. Additional thanks should be bestowed on the chefs who saw potential in their home city and returned here to add their voices to an ever-deepening culinary conversation, not to mention those who ventured here from abroad and saw the promise of a young scene with infinite opportunity. Without these forerunners, the city would not be what it has become.

Today, although a modicum of the shadow remains, Milwaukee has largely come into its own as a city bursting with cultural outlets, well-groomed parks, a fine zoo, superb natural history and art museums and an endless stream of year-round festivals. And its food scene—proudly devoid of chains—has blossomed into an evolving cornucopia of diverse restaurant options. It is largely driven by chefs whose respect for Wisconsin's agricultural bounty and passion for creativity provide the city with wide-ranging options for nourishment and community. It is also a rising star in terms of its contributions to urban food production and farming, an asset to both the environmental health of the city and the food scene itself.

With the exception of Los Angeles and New York City, Milwaukee has opened more successful restaurants per capita during the recent economic downturn than any other city in the nation. That growth—paired with an increasing number of educated, adventurous diners—has created an atmosphere of optimism and excitement in dining that is likely to continue to perpetuate additional growth in the industry.

No longer a city on the fringe of the "big leagues," Milwaukee has become a culinary destination worthy of notice. And this is its story.

Beginnings

Before Milwaukee became a dining town, food production was at the fore of its industry. But it wasn't bratwurst and beer that fueled Milwaukee's first settlers. It was land.

Prior to the nineteenth century, Native American tribes—including the Menominee, Fox, Potawatomi and Ho-Chunk—were the sole inhabitants of the Milwaukee area. In fact, the name Milwaukee is derived from the Algonquian word *Millioke*, which roughly translates to "good, beautiful and pleasant land." Of the tribes, the most influential in southeastern Wisconsin was the Potawatomi. However, when French explorers first ventured into the territory in the late seventeenth and eighteenth centuries, the native population declined rapidly after succumbing to diseases brought here from Europe.

Jacques Vieau, a French Canadian trader and occupant of Green Bay, is largely considered to be the first resident of Milwaukee. Although he did not live in the area year round, he established a fur trading post from which he dealt with local tribes from 1795 through the 1830s.

The first settlers arrived in Milwaukee in the early 1800s with farming on their minds. They cleared forests and drained swamps, forming three immigrant towns—Juneautown, Kilbourntown and Walker's Point—that would merge in the 1840s to become a unified city. And soon, due to their efforts, wheat became the bumper crop that put the area on the map.

In the mid-nineteenth century, Milwaukee earned the nickname "Cream City," a nod to the large number of cream-colored bricks fired in

Milwaukee Feeds the World poster print. *Author's collection.*

the Menomonee River Valley and used in construction. At its peak, the city produced 15 million bricks per year, with one-third going out of state. But it was the city's ethnic populations that would influence the direction of its development. By 1860, Germans made up the majority, followed by Polish, Irish and eastern European immigrants. The city

The Daisy Roller Mill, originally called the Kilbourn Mill, produced a capacity of 1,800 barrels of flour daily in the 1850s. *Author's collection*.

had more than two dozen breweries dotting the city, sponsoring beer gardens throughout.

In a shift from commerce to manufacturing during the late 1880s, meatpacking took over as the city's largest industry, allowing businesses like Patrick Cudahy to thrive. Milwaukee's most famous sausage producer, Usinger's, was founded in 1880. Meanwhile, in the 1890s, Sicilian immigrants perfected the wholesale produce market, while others started businesses making pasta and other traditional Italian foods. Chinese immigrants, largely from Canton, established Chinese laundries and restaurants as early as 1874. And Polish immigrants, who arrived in the mid- to late 1800s, established bakeries, butcher shops and other outfits on Milwaukee's South Side in neighborhoods that would also house Hispanic immigrants a half century later.

All the while, Wisconsin was becoming an agricultural powerhouse. By the late 1800s, Milwaukee was the second-largest producer of wheat in the country, with the biggest wheat exchange in the world. Grain elevators dominated the Milwaukee skyline, and flourmills became the heart of industry. This early success helped Wisconsin's agriculture develop more rapidly than it did in other states. As competition from farmers in Iowa and Minnesota increased, feed crops quickly surpassed wheat. By the mid-nineteenth century, dairying emerged as the most viable alternative to wheat. By 1899, nearly all of Wisconsin farms raised dairy cows.

As Wisconsin's largest city, Milwaukee soon became the hub for barley, wheat flour and meat products. And by the beginning of the twentieth century, the Cream City would also start a long journey in establishing a flourishing dining scene.

Hotel Dining

Hotels quickly found a local market in Milwaukee's earliest days. After all, waves of land speculators and settlers needed places to stay and, inevitably, to dine.

THE NEWHALL HOUSE

Milwaukee's first upscale hotel, and one of the most magnificent in the United States, was the Newhall House, built by merchant Daniel Newhall in 1856 at 611 North Broadway in 1856. The three-hundred-room hotel was an imposing structure for its day, boasting six stories; its restaurant, which offered *table d'hote (prix fixe)* dining, also featured an extensive wine list. An early menu touted, "Meals will be prompt, and no gong sounded."

Unfortunately, the Newhall House's beautiful brick exterior belied a secret. Its wood-frame structure and gaslights, both standard for its time, made it prone to fire. The building sustained blazes in both 1863 and 1880 before being destroyed by fire in January 1883. But in the year before its demise, the hotel gave rise to the Milwaukee Club, a dining and social hot spot that eventually established its own home at 706 North Jefferson Street.

THE PFISTER

Pfister Hotel. *Courtesy of the Marcus Corporation Archives.*

Future hotels took extra precautions. At the time of its completion in 1893, the Pfister Hotel (424 West Wisconsin Avenue) had already gained iconic status as being one of the first all-electric, completely fireproof hotels. With two hundred guest rooms, sixty-one private bathrooms and fourteen baths, the "Grand Hotel of the West" opened to worldwide critical acclaim.

Dining at the Pfister was always an attraction. The English Room opened in 1926 as a pub that served steaks and chops. During the 1930s and '40s, Milwaukee's most prominent citizens frequently gathered there.

After Ben Marcus purchased the hotel in 1962, the restaurant was renovated and evolved into a steakhouse, switching over to high-end dining in the 1970s and French and nouvelle fare the following decade. But the staff never abandoned its dedication to superb food and fine service.

Until 2001, when the English Room was reinvented as Celia, a more contemporary restaurant, presidents and dignitaries from around the world made regular visits to the Pfister, where they could enjoy elegant classics such as filet mignon, roast rack of lamb and fresh salmon amid an impressive collection of original nineteenth- and early twentieth-century artwork.

Today, diners can enjoy breakfast or lunch in casual elegance at Café at the Pfister or dinner at Mason Street Grill, which specializes in wood-grilled steaks. The Pfister's legendary Sunday brunch is served in the Rouge, one of the hotel's remaining historic dining areas. A special feature, offered only during the fall and winter months, is weekend afternoon tea service, complete with the hospitality of a tea butler.

The Schroeder

In 1927, Walter Schroeder—owner of two other Milwaukee hotels, Astor Hotel and Hotel Wisconsin—built the Schroeder Hotel, which was at the time both the tallest and largest hotel in the state.

The original hotel contained a cocktail lounge and coffee shop, as well as a private breakfast room named after Schroeder's niece, Lorraine. Dinner was served in the majestic Empire Room, which boasted a lovely view of Wisconsin Avenue. The hotel played host to many chefs over the years, including John Marangelli, who had trained in Italy and would later mentor Paul Bartolotta.

Photo of the Hotel Schroeder in the 1950s. *Courtesy of the Marcus Corporation Archives.*

HOTEL SCHROEDER
MILWAUKEE, WIS.

Midnight Specialties

Served after 11 o'clock

•

Toasted Snappy Wisconsin Cheese Sandwich	.20
Deviled Smithfield's Virginia Ham - - -	.25
On Rye Bread	
Olive and Nut - - - - - - - - -	.20
On Toasted Roll	
Denver Sandwich, Sliced Tomato,	
Sweet Pickle - - - - - - - -	.20
Beef Steak, Tartare, on Milwaukee Rye -	.30
Chopped Spanish Onions	
Chicken Salad Canape - - - - - -	.30
Mayonnaise Dressing, Hard Boiled Egg	
Scotch Woodcock - - - - - - - -	.30
Scrambled Egg and Anchovy on Toast	

•

(For Other Suggestions Please Ask for A La Carte Menu)
(Please Do Not Request Substitutions)

COCKTAIL LOUNGE
(ONLY)

Late-night menu from the Hotel Schroeder Cocktail Lounge, circa late 1940s. *Courtesy of the Marcus Corporation Archives.*

After Schroeder sold the hotel in 1967, it became a Sheraton. In 1972, the hotel was sold to Ben and Steve Marcus, who renamed the building the Marc Plaza and subsequently franchised it as a Hilton in 1995. Today, the Hilton boasts two restaurants: the Milwaukee ChopHouse and the Miller Time Pub, as well as the Café, a casual breakfast spot, and Monarch Lounge, which offers cocktails, food and live jazz in the evening. The Lorraine Room now functions as a private lounge and dining space for Hilton Honors guests.

The Ambassador

In 1928, during the Art Deco movement, Milwaukee architects Urban Peacock and Armin Frank graced the city with yet another hotel. The Ambassador, located at 2308 West Wisconsin Avenue, was created in prime Art Deco form, with a blend of craft motif and Machine Age imagery flavored with the "Egyptomania" of the era. It's largely the building's distinct style that still attracts tourists and diners to the historic spot.

In the 1930s, lounge patrons were regularly entertained by the piano stylings of West Allis native Walter Busterkeys, the pianist who would eventually become nationally known as Liberace. In 1964, the Beatles took Milwaukee by storm and spent a night at the Ambassador Hotel, which made the news when it was surrounded by hundreds of adoring fans.

Unfortunately, by the 1970s, the neighborhood surrounding the hotel had fallen into decline and the hotel was remodeled as a low-end residence. Rough times followed as Jeffrey Dahmer committed his second of seventeen murders—his first in Milwaukee—in one of the Ambassador's guest rooms in 1987.

Fortunately, all was not lost. In 2013, after a ten-year, $14 million restoration by owner Rick Wiegand, the Ambassador was returned to its former glory. From the original marble floors and bronze elevator doors to the ornate plasterwork, every detail of the Ambassador Hotel is a testament to the bold beauty of Art Deco. Today's Ambassador houses the Envoy Restaurant and Lounge, an upscale yet casual eatery. Its American-style cuisine is made with locally grown, seasonal ingredients, including a unique made-to-order small-plate brunch and a "buy one, get one at the 1928 price" happy hour promotion. Meanwhile, Caffe Deco features grab-and-go breakfast and lunch options, including baked goods, soup and salads.

Although dining has migrated largely to independent eateries, Milwaukee hotels—whether new or well established—still cater to a local dining population. Historic spots like the Knick, located at the Knickerbocker on the Lake on Juneau Avenue, regularly attract neighborhood breakfast and brunch crowds, particularly during the summer months, when they can enjoy the outdoor patio overlooking Lake Michigan. The restaurant at Hotel Metro, a former downtown office building that was transformed into an eco-friendly Art Moderne hotel in 1998, has been home to numerous local chefs, including Mike Engel, current owner of Bay View's Pastiche. Meanwhile, Smyth, a newer eatery located at the Iron Horse Hotel in Walker's Point, has been named among "8 of the Most Delicious Farm-to-Table Hotels in the World" by Yahoo Travel. The Yard, its sprawling urban patio, attracts the attention of tourists and locals alike as a popular spot for treats and tipples on warm, breezy afternoons.

A Century of Eateries

Prior to Prohibition, most restaurants in this city of breweries were taverns. And it seems only natural that most specialized in German fare. Forst-Keller, the Steubenhof, the Old Heidelberg, Fritz Gust Café Restaurant and Ritter's Inn were well known and well loved in their times, but by the 1960s, Milwaukee was known for its "Big Three": John Ernst Café, Mader's and Karl Ratzsch's.

JOHN ERNST CAFÉ

John Ernst Café, long billed as the oldest restaurant in Wisconsin, began in 1878 as Mother Heister's Place, a two-story brick saloon with a beer garden. By 1938, the eatery at 600 East Ogden Avenue had become known as the Ogden Café, and Hungarian immigrant John Ernst, who worked there as a waiter, had become the owner.

Thanks to his wife Ida's deft hand in the kitchen, the café became known for its schnitzels, *rouladen*, whole roast duck, smoked pork chops and veal *paprikash*. Its sauerbraten was made the old-fashioned way, marinated for three days with hand-blended spices.

For decades, John Ernst's interior paid homage to the Old World with murals of café society, warm wooden paneling, an impressive stone fireplace, leaded-glass windows and a timbered ceiling festooned with heavy iron chandeliers amid bucks' antlers.

John Ernst Café, circa 1940. *Author's collection.*

The café, which was passed on through the family—first to the Ernsts' daughter, Marianne, and then to her sons, Jim and John—was included on top restaurant lists through the 1990s. The restaurant closed in 2001 and is now home to Karma Bar & Grill, a sports bar known for its burgers. The new restaurant pays homage to the location's history by displaying the original 1878 wooden door above the large original fireplace on the main floor.

MADER'S

In 1902, Charles Mader spent his life savings on a small building on Plankinton Avenue and named it the Comfort. For twenty cents (including tip), a customer could enjoy dinner, which included a large stein of Cream City beer. A few years later, Mader moved the restaurant to its current location, 1041 North Old World Third Street, renamed it Mader's and launched the restaurant to national fame.

A firm believer in the power of advertising, Mader often remarked, "If your business is not worth advertising, advertise it for sale." And his actions followed suit. In 1929, a short newspaper feature suspiciously resembling an advertorial claimed that Mader's had won a reputation for hospitality extending "the length and breadth of this land and to distant lands as well."

During Prohibition, as Mader shifted focus from German beer to food, both locals and tourists flocked to the restaurant to indulge in sauerkraut balls and *spätzle*, *krautflecken*, liver dumpling soup and several types of schnitzel, including Count Esterhazy, Black Forest, Ritter and Innsbruck à la Holstein.

With the help of his sons, George and Gustave, Mader ushered the restaurant through the aftermath of World War II—and its anti-German backlash—by downplaying the German theme. But once the bitterness had subsided, Mader's again became a haven for German food lovers. Visiting celebrities hung their autographed photos on the walls, and accolades rolled in. Mader's began to win awards and listings in national magazines and restaurant guides such as Duncan Hines's *Adventures in Good Eating* and those of the Automobile Club of America and Ford Motor Company.

In the 1930s, the Maders remodeled the Third Street building to more closely resemble a German medieval villa, sporting a high-stepped gable and two bas-relief panels depicting costumed servers. Subsequent remodels added a vaulted ceiling decorated with swords and shields and a new dining room.

In the early '70s, Mader's foyer became, for a few short years, a miniature art gallery. In 1977, the operations were moved to the second floor of the Milwaukee restaurant and, from 1980 to the present, to the Tower Galleries. Today's diners sit amid a stunning $3 million collection of art, medieval suits of armor and relics dating back to the fourteenth century. By 2002, Mader's was awarded status as the world's largest Hummel store. To this day, Mader's continues to be honored as one of Milwaukee's best ethnic restaurants.

KARL RATZSCH'S

While John Ernst's took credit for being the oldest German restaurant and Mader's became the best known, Karl Ratzsch's is the one German eatery that focused on fine dining.

Ratzsch's Restaurant began in 1904, when Chef Otto Hermann opened Hermann's Café on Water Street in downtown Milwaukee, which he ran with the help of his stepdaughter, Helen. In 1929, after a ten-year courtship, Helen married Karl August Ratzsch Sr., and they purchased the café, relocating it to 320 East Mason Street and renaming it Karl Ratzsch's. The

Karl Ratzsch's *Holiday Magazine* postcard, circa 1952. *Author's collection.*

two continued operation for decades before passing the reins to Karl Jr., who carried on the restaurant's successful tradition into the 1990s, when he sold the restaurant to his son, Josef. The restaurant remained in the Ratzsch family until 2003, when Josef sold it to Executive Chef John Poulos, restaurant manager Tom Andera and dining room manager Judy Hazard.

Karl Ratzsch's has won countless awards and honors, including the *Travel Holiday Magazine* Award, a spot among *USA Today*'s "10 Best Restaurants in the U.S." list and a place in the DiRoNA Hall of Fame.

These days, Karl Ratzsch's tends to be a destination for Milwaukee visitors, especially those interested in trying authentic German food. The restaurant greets visitors with cozy wood paneling and walls dotted with oil paintings in ornate golden frames. "Mama" Ratzsch's collection of steins, porcelain and glassware decorate the back bar and plate rails around the room.

The menu features specialties like *käse spätzle*, a savory strudel stuffed with smoked pork and cheese; a variety of wursts and schnitzels; *konigsberger klopse* and goulash; and sauerkraut, red cabbage and potato dumplings, German potato salad and consommé with liver dumplings. Homemade strudels, *schaum* torte and puffy German pancakes stand out among the desserts.

Global Cuisines

In addition to its German cuisine, for which Milwaukee would become famous, the city also played host to a wide variety of flavors, including American, Chinese, French and eastern European. Whether trendsetters or Milwaukee classics, some would sustain themselves for nearly a century, and all would play a role in putting the Cream City on the national dining map.

Kalt's Restaurant

Milwaukee's Kalt family made their mark as restaurateurs, owning and operating establishments dating back to the mid-1800s. These spaces included Joseph P. Kalt's downtown saloon on Grand Avenue (now Wisconsin Avenue) and two restaurants near the Pabst Theater, both of which were managed by family members. But the eatery at 2856 North Oakland Avenue, owned by Henry Kalt, is the one most Milwaukeeans remember. By the time his son, Howard, took over in 1948, it had become an East Side institution.

The walls of Kalt's Restaurant were covered with caricatures of stars who had played at the J. Pellman Theatre next door, as well as Howard's large collection of breweriana—including knobs, beer trays, bottles and labels. By the 1960s, the restaurant was serving dishes like filet mignon, fried shrimp and scallops and lobster tail, plus fried fish on Fridays. Howard ran the restaurant until he retired. The space was sold in 1985, becoming Oakland Trattoria and, later, Black Rose Irish Pub. It would eventually go down in history as being the location of Chef Sanford D'Amato's first industry job, where he worked the line making sandwiches and breading fish for the Friday fish fry.

Watts Tea Shop

It was 1901 when Elizabeth Bigelow and her sister, Caroline Bigelow McGeoch, established a teashop on Mason Street in downtown Milwaukee. The shop was one of many tearooms—most owned and operated by women—that had begun taking hold in the United States. The phenomenon, which exploded in popularity during the 1920s, marked a moment when women's suffrage, Prohibition and increased female independence came together to lay the groundwork for today's smaller restaurants and coffee bars.

After ten years in business, the Bigelow sisters relinquished their ownership, and another set of sisters, Marie and Amelia Cook, took over management of the tearoom, renaming it Cook's Tea Shop. The shop operated on Mason Street until 1929, when it moved to the second floor of the George Watts & Son building at 761 North Jefferson Street. The restaurant kept the Cook's Tea Shop moniker until the mid-1930s, when management converted over to Watts.

Today, the Watts Tea Shop, which serves breakfast and lunch and hosts private tea events, remains a second-story fixture with a bright, light-filled dining area and formal décor. It is said that numerous recipes served there date back to the 1930s, including the olive-nut and chicken salad finger sandwiches; the wheat bread and English muffins, baked daily; and its locally renowned Sunshine Cake, three layers of lemon chiffon filled with French custard and iced with seven-minute frosting.

In 2011, the Watts Tea Shop was honored by the James Beard Foundation as one of "America's Classics," a recognition bestowed on restaurants with "timeless appeal, beloved for quality food that reflects the character of their community."

Toy's

Just as restaurants like Mader's and Karl Ratzsch's were seeing their beginnings, Chinese restaurants were also popping up around Milwaukee. One of the most popular was Toy's.

Founded by Moy Toy Ni—or Charlie Toy, as he came to be known—the restaurant opened on what is now Plankinton Avenue in 1904. Toy, who had come to the United States from Canton in 1880 and worked for Karl Ratzsch's before opening his own place, gained popularity for his chop suey, pressed duck and other Chinese dishes.

By 1913, Toy's restaurant and other business ventures had become successful enough that he was able to move the restaurant to a six-story Chinese architectural–style building. Designed by Alexander Guth, the Second Street building also housed a movie theater, Hascall Billiard Parlor and a few small commercial businesses. By 1946, it had been demolished, and Toy's son, Moy, relocated the restaurant to Wisconsin Avenue and, later, to Old World Third Street, where it remained until it closed in 2000.

Milwaukee's Chinese population was largely dispersed, with no Chinatown or a unified wider Asian community. But while Toy's was flashier than most, it would play an important role in contributing to Milwaukee's Asian dining scene.

Eugene's Seafood Restaurant

"The Sign of the Lobster" marked the location of Eugene's Seafood Restaurant at 811 East Wisconsin Avenue. The restaurant, established in 1919 by Eugene G. Trimberger, will go down in history as being the only Milwaukee restaurant to rate a Duncan Hines award for a quarter of a century.

Trimberger, who was known for the elaborate dinners he presented while managing at the Milwaukee Club, focused the Eugene's menu on lobster, Pacific crab, oysters and clams, along with a raw spinach salad—items that pleased his higher-end clientele.

Trimberger owned and managed the restaurant and operated the Juneau Hotel until 1959, when he turned the restaurant over to Morris Friedman so he could take over full-time management of the hotel. A bleak 1971 review by Herbert Kubley in the *Milwaukee Journal* described the "ocean-fresh Maine lobster" as "dry and flat" and the baked potato as "soggy and leaden"—a possible indicator that the restaurant was declining. It closed in 1974.

Frenchy's Café

By the 1940s, Milwaukee's food scene was growing quickly enough to accommodate an increasing number of novelty restaurants. One such spot was Frenchy's Café & Le Cabaret (1827 East North Avenue), which quickly gained a reputation as one of Milwaukee's best.

Owned by Paul LaPointe, Frenchy's was recognized both nationally and internationally for its exotic game, French service and ambience, earning the Holiday Award and recommendations from Duncan Hines, AAA and the Gourmet Club.

In 1951, according to an article published in the *Milwaukee Sentinel*, internationally known food and wine columnist Maurice C. Dreicer gave the restaurant props for its perfectly prepared steak and sent an elaborately engraved silver butter knife to the restaurant along with a note reading, "The steak I ate at Frenchy's was cut with a similar knife."

In an OnMilwaukee.com article from 2006, the late Dr. Ron Snyder waxed poetic about the restaurant, describing it as

> *a dimly lit, overly decorated spot complete with red velvet wallpaper and plush red carpeting. It featured a few private dining booths shielded from the crowd by red velvet curtains. The bar was of highly polished wood running*

nearly the length of the establishment and featured lots of exotic umbrella drinks. The entrées were equally unusual and included such delicacies as ostrich and something passing for some kind of bear meat. I must admit that I did not have the nerve to try either and stuck with the tried-and-true steak at the outrageous price of about $10.95 per meal. As I recall, the food was served a la carte, and one could easily run up a bill of $15 or $20 with salad and soup.

Before his death in 1981, LaPointe would also run two other restaurants, Paul's Small Café (1854 East Kenilworth Place) and the Fleur de Lis, in Milwaukee's Cudahy Towers, a French fine dining restaurant that he managed from 1957 to 1960.

The Boulevard Inn

When the original location of the Boulevard Inn (4300 West Lloyd Street) burned to the ground in February 1993, there was an outcry from the dining public. Although the restaurant had moved to Cudahy Towers on the East Side the year before, the building had become a reminder of more elegant times. It was the harbinger of fond memories—weddings, celebrations and bar mitzvahs—as well as a go-to neighborhood restaurant. It was a destination for both locals and luminaries, including the Harleys and the Davidsons of Milwaukee motorcycle fame and comedienne Phyllis Diller, who is said to have stopped by whenever she was in town.

The Boulevard Inn, which opened in 1946, was an elegant choice for a special evening out. However, it was also a comfortable neighborhood spot where people stopped for a sundae, a club sandwich or a late-night cocktail. The Boulevard Inn was first situated with a scenic view of Washington Park and its bronze statue of Baron Friedrich Wilhelm von Steuben, the Prussian hero of the American Revolutionary War. Formerly the home of the Steubenhof, a German restaurant and tavern, the building was purchased by Marie and Albert Gaulke, restaurateurs who had run the Chesterfield Grill on Juneau Avenue, as well as Gaulke's Coffee Shop near the Riverside Theater downtown.

For many years, the Gaulkes employed a German chef, Friedel Emmerich, who had been a prisoner of war held at Milwaukee's Mitchell Field during World War II. Emmerich's menu featured German classics including sauerbraten, roulade and goulash, as well as steak, lobster, liver pâté and shrimp cocktail. The Caesar salad and honey duck, both made tableside, were legendary. For dessert, the specialty was *schaum* torte with strawberries or *Pashka* with raspberry Melba sauce.

In 1968, the Gaulkes sold the restaurant to son-in-law Werner Strothmann, who ran it with sons Gary and Mark until 1992, when changes to the neighborhood prompted them to move the restaurant to the former Fleur de Lis space in Cudahy Towers. When his father suffered a stroke that same year, Gary Strothmann took over management of the restaurant until it closed in 2003. The site would become home to Bartolotta's Bacchus the following year.

Three Brothers

In the 1950s, Milwaukee got a taste of Serbian food when Milun Radicevic opened Three Brothers at 2414 South Saint Clair Street. Radicevic, a Holocaust survivor who landed in Wisconsin after being sponsored by a Milwaukee family, named the restaurant for his three sons, whom he hoped would join him from Yugoslavia.

One of his sons, Branko, arrived in America a few years later to make a life for himself, attending school, living on both coasts and starting a family. But in 1972, he came to Milwaukee to help run the family business and assumed the role of manager in 1975. Branko would remain with the restaurant, bringing smiles and hospitality to guests in the dining room, until his death in 2014.

Three Brothers served eastern European favorites like stuffed peppers, goulash and roast goose, as well as börek, a spinach-cheese pie made with phyllo. The restaurant, often described as "homey" and "cozy," was included on *Milwaukee Journal-Sentinel* food critic Carol Deptolla's "Top 30" list. It was also featured in *Bon Appétit* and *Gourmet* and on the Food Network. But a highlight for the family came in 2002, when Three Brothers won a James Beard Award as an "American Classic." Today, the giant Schlitz globe atop the building still serves as a beacon for those seeking out old-world charm in the form of authentic Serbian fare.

Old Town Serbian Gourmet House

Eventually, all three of Milun Radicevic's sons would assist him in operating his Three Brothers restaurant. One son, Alexander, who had come to

Milwaukee in 1959, worked for his father for a number of years before opening his own restaurant with his wife, Radmila.

Old Town Serbian Gourmet House opened its doors in 1971 in a former tavern and bowling alley at 522 West Lincoln Avenue. Originally named Stari Grad, a historic area in the capital city of Belgrade, the restaurant's name was later changed to the English translation: Old Town. Its interior paid homage to the old country with a collection of Yugoslavian art, including a commissioned mural of Belgrade by Yugoslavian émigré Slobodan Laschich.

Alexander managed the front of the house, while Radmila took the helm in the kitchen, creating traditional, from-scratch Serbian dishes including tripe marinated in sour cream, chicken *paprikash*, goulash, *cevapcici* (Serbian sausage), *raznjici* (kabobs), *sarma* (stuffed cabbage) and beef börek (pastry filled with seasoned beef).

A fire gutted much of the business in 1976, but Alexander rebuilt in ten weeks with the help of friends and family. Although the original murals were destroyed, he gradually rebuilt his collection of Yugoslavia-oriented art.

In 2010, after forty years in business, Alexander and Radmila handed off the business to their daughter, Natalia, who purchased and remodeled the original building in 2013. Despite many updates, the restaurant continues to provide Milwaukeeans with solidly authentic cuisine in an atmosphere that feels like a step back in time.

THE MILWAUKEE FOOD SCENE GROWS

By 1963, a headline in the July 4 edition of the *Milwaukee Sentinel* would laud the city as being "famed for good food," citing the exciting variety of steakhouses, Italian restaurants, German food and a "smorgasbord" of choices for eager diners. The same issue of the paper held advertisements for countless restaurants, including Alioto's, the Beehive Supper Club, Highland House, Howard Johnson's, Como's and Fazio's on Jackson.

The 1970s would bring additional acclaim with the visit of food writer and critic Roy Andries de Groot. According to an article by Don Oleson in the April 19, 1970 edition of the *Milwaukee Journal*, De Groot rated the city very high, "almost on a level with San Francisco, except for the lack of a high cuisine French restaurant." During his visit, De Groot is also said to have passed blame on the State of Wisconsin for failing to promote Milwaukee's food along with its beer.

Seven years later, De Groot returned to Milwaukee and sang the praises of Karl Ratzsch's, Jean-Paul Restaurant Francais, Old Town Serbian Gourmet House, Three Brothers and Kalt's. According to *Milwaukee Sentinel* author Dorothy Kinkaid, the gourmand also showed respect for the midwestern hospitality and work ethic evident in the city's restaurants, saying that he noted "a discipline, a sense of service. People seem to do their best here, they struggle to get the best possible ingredients. There seems to be less of a profit motive, in the greedy sense."

Jean-Paul Restaurant Francais

By 1975, De Groot's wish would come to pass, as Chef Jean-Paul Weber, native of Alsace, France, established Jean-Paul Restaurant Francais at 811 East Wisconsin Avenue. Weber, who worked in a variety of European kitchens, including Maxim's in Paris, came to America in 1964 to work at Maxim's in Chicago. He also cooked at the Flying Frenchman and Chez Paul there before opening Chez Paul–Willowbrook in Thiensville in 1972.

Jean-Paul Restaurant Francais took the place of Milwaukee's Eugene's, transforming the décor to reflect a French country theme. Specials included breast of chicken Oscar, tenderloin Milanese and *escalope* Normandy, along with roast rack of lamb. The restaurant also served lunch, including the beloved duo Croque Monsieur and Croque Madame, along with other sandwiches and salads.

In 1981, the restaurant would change directions, becoming La Brasserie, a spot with a more modestly priced menu, plus a small upscale dining area he called Jean-Paul's Gourmet Room.

Marangelli's

Chef John Marangelli made his stamp on Milwaukee as one of its foremost Italian chefs. Marangelli, who grew up and trained in Florence, Italy, came to the United States in the early 1960s. Noted for his work at the Schroeder/ Sheraton Hotel, Marangelli then opened a series of restaurants bearing his name, including Marangelli's al Lago (777 East Michigan Avenue).

During the 1980s, he took high-end Italian dining to a new level at his restaurant in the Holiday Inn at 5423 North Port Washington Road, presenting diners with seventeen-course *festas*, Italian gourmet feasts that included delicacies like roast rooster breast and supreme of rabbit and eel. Before Marangelli's death in 2002, he provided tutelage for numerous Milwaukee chefs, including Chef Paul Bartolotta, who would go on to open Ristorante Bartolotta with his brother, Joe, in 1993 and win two James Beard Awards for his work at Bartolotta Ristorante di Mare in Las Vegas.

Grenadier's

Many Milwaukee food enthusiasts trace the beginnings of the modern restaurant scene back to one restaurant: Grenadier's. In 1978, Fran Zell of the *Chicago Tribune* wrote, "With all its fine dining rooms, Chicago has nothing, except perhaps for its exclusive private clubs, quite like Milwaukee's Grenadier's."

Launched in 1975 by Robert Jordan and Knut Apitz, the restaurant was considered one of Milwaukee's finest and was known for its contemporary cuisine. During its heyday in the 1980s, the restaurant, which was located at 747 North Broadway, set the standard for fine dining in Milwaukee as a special-occasion destination for those who appreciated fine food and impeccable service. Grenadier's represented a style of dining found only in Michelin-starred restaurants in Europe. That meant white tablecloths, dark-suited waiters and menu items like sweetbreads, wild boar, venison and Tournedos Rossini.

German-born Apitz began his career as an apprentice at a restaurant in Berlin before graduating from *Berufsschule*, a German culinary program. "Early in my career," he noted, "a chef advised me to try to work in the finest places I could get in to get as much experience as I could."

Apitz took the advice to heart, working in numerous positions in Germany, Holland, England and Switzerland before moving to Milwaukee to work at the Tripoli Country Club and opening Grenadier's. He was generous with his knowledge and passed along his experience and skill to numerous chefs who worked alongside him. Chefs like Joe Muench of Black Shoe Hospitality remained in Milwaukee and made names for themselves here, while others went on to pursue their careers nationally.

At Grenadier's, Apitz was well known for his ability to whip up delicious dishes on the fly. In addition to a standard menu, he would entertain special requests from diners, often serving as many off-the-cuff specials as regular restaurant offerings. It was all a part of his dedication to excellent customer service. "If you came in and you had a wish, we wouldn't say, 'No, we don't do that,'" said Apitz. "We would say, 'Yes, ma'am' or 'Yes, sir.'"

He recalled entertaining a group of businessmen from New York in the 1980s. As they talked, one of the men challenged Apitz. "I have the urge for an elephant ear on a bun," the man noted. Apitz's retort was classic: "I'm sorry, but we are out of buns."

Apitz was also known for his imaginative dishes, as well as his creative use of off-cuts like sweetbreads, veal tongue and veal brains. On one particular evening, Apitz recalled, he entertained a number of his colleagues during the food show, which was taking place at Milwaukee's Mecca Arena. As a main course, he prepared a roasted peacock, which he expertly displayed atop the bird's plumage. The dish was so spectacular that when carted through the dining room, it received myriad *oohs* and *ahhs* from customers.

In the mid-'80s, Apitz hosted the very first benefit dinner for Milwaukee's Ronald McDonald House, which provides living quarters for families of children who are receiving critical medical care at Children's Hospital. Under his direction, the Annual Chefs' Dinner became a tradition, sometimes involving as many as sixty chefs for each dinner. They continue today, now led by Muench.

Apitz's efforts won him the affection of many, including a range of professional associations to which he belonged. In 1993, Apitz won Wisconsin Restaurant Association's Chef of the Year, followed by honors as Chef of the Year by the American Culinary Federation in 1994. As of 1996, Grenadier's was the only restaurant in Milwaukee to receive a four-star rating from the *Mobil Travel Guide*, a national guide to restaurants and hotels. In 2010, the American Culinary Federation of Chefs of Milwaukee presented him with a lifetime achievement award.

A fire in Grenadier's kitchen in July 2001 forced it to close for seven months. It reopened in February 2002, featuring a new interior and new menu, but it never regained its previous traction. Nonetheless, Grenadier's, which closed for good in 2004, would go down in history as opening the door for a new sort of dining in Milwaukee.

John Byron's

In 1978, when John Byron's replaced Bennigan's Restaurant in the First Wisconsin Center (777 East Wisconsin Avenue), owner John Byron Burns, vice-president of Heinemann's Restaurants, intended for it to be a "$5.95 pre-theater place." But over the years, the restaurant emerged as one of Milwaukee's most elegant, a phenomenon that could be largely attributed to the influence of Executive Chef Sanford D'Amato, the one-time line cook at Kalt's.

D'Amato, who had returned to Milwaukee from studying in New York in 1979, revised the menu at John Byron's, putting an emphasis on fresh, simple fare, including seafood. At the time, D'Amato recalled, there weren't many trendy restaurants in Milwaukee. But Burns gave him creative license over the menu, and D'Amato took the restaurant to new heights. As the 1980s saw the birth of California cuisine at restaurants like Mustard's and Michael Chiarello's Tra Vigne, Burns developed an interest. With D'Amato's help, they hosted a series of California wine dinners. It was something new for Milwaukee, something that pushed the media to take notice.

During his tenure at John Byron's, D'Amato received national attention. In 1985, *Food and Wine* magazine named him one of the "25 Hot New Chefs." Three years later, *Bon Appétit* touted him as one of the finest seafood chefs in the country, and he was selected as one of twelve national finalists in the American Culinary Gold Cup, Bocuse d'Or.

D'Amato departed in 1989 to open his own restaurant, Sanford, largely contributing to the decline of John Byron's, which closed in 1991. But D'Amato's legacy would live on, prompting a sea change in the Milwaukee dining scene.

The Start of Something Big

Milwaukee had finally earned a place in the fine dining scene, mainly thanks to chefs who were emulating the great Escoffier's French style. But it wasn't until the 1980s that the Cream City really reached its culinary coming of age.

SANFORD

In 1970, young Sanford D'Amato left Milwaukee to attend culinary school at the brand-new Hyde Park Culinary Institute of America in New York. It was a move that, unbeknownst to him at the time, would eventually change the face of Milwaukee dining forever. "I didn't think I was ever coming back," said D'Amato. "I had no plans to come back. I figured I'd be working on the West Coast or, ideally, in New York."

D'Amato grew up in Milwaukee, where his father and grandfather operated a grocery store for nearly eighty years. His grandfather, like so many other Italians, cured his own olives and made wine in his basement. And his mother knew her way around the kitchen. D'Amato began his career working in area restaurants, but deep down, he knew that he wanted more than what Milwaukee could offer.

In Hyde Park, he came under the tutelage of Peter von Erp, a mentor he described as both a madman and a genius. D'Amato became the first

Sanford and Angela D'Amato. *Photo by Kevin J. Miyazaki.*

American cook at Le Veau d'Or and worked under Chef Roland Chenus through the groundbreaking opening of Le Chantilly. But it was a stint working in Long Island that made him decide to return home. "Long Island in the fall—during the off-season—was like living in a small town," D'Amato said. "We developed a real connection with the local people. And it reminded me of things I missed about Milwaukee."

A 1920s photo of the D'Amato family grocery store and future home of Sanford. *Courtesy of Sandy and Angie D'Amato. Copy/documentation of photo by Kevin J. Miyazaki.*

On his occasional trips home, D'Amato witnessed changes in the local scene. Chefs like Knut Apitz were making headway with high-end cuisine, and D'Amato started to contemplate the possibility of moving back and starting a restaurant, something he never envisioned being able to do in New York.

In 1980, D'Amato returned to Milwaukee, where he took a job working at John Byron's, the place he credits with solidifying his reputation locally, as well as the spot he met his future wife and partner, Angie Provencher. The D'Amato family grocery had mostly run its course, so in 1989, Sandy and Angie bought the building at 1547 North Jackson Street, moved in upstairs and began converting the store to a restaurant. After three months of frantic activity, Sanford opened on December 7.

The opening was a disaster, but the next day was better. The staff stayed up until 3:00 a.m. finding answers to first night's glitches. From there, Sanford started attracting attention immediately. *Esquire* named it one of the top new restaurants of 1990. Soon after, D'Amato was one of twelve chefs Julia Child invited to cook for her eightieth birthday celebration.

But the acclaim didn't come without hard work. For years, both Sandy and Angie worked from 6:00 a.m. to midnight, six days a week. Sandy held down the fort in the kitchen, and Angie handled the front of the house, a team effort Sandy said contributed directly to their success. "She gave me the freedom to do what I did best," he says, "and created an atmosphere of service that was pretty inerrable."

It took four years, said D'Amato, before he felt comfortable taking a day off from the restaurant. And even then, he devoted his free time to travel and building up his culinary knowledge. "For a lot of years, the competition in the city was the city itself," he noted. "People, restaurants, just were not putting themselves on a global map. But from the time we opened, we were always looking at what others were doing around the world."

International influence showed in the menus. There was a grilled pear and Roquefort tart with caramelized onions, weathervane scallops with lobster broth and long-bean seaweed, Chilean sea bass and Yu Choy ravioli with glazed garlic and orange zest gremolata and also char-grilled loin of elk with chestnut-celeriac puree and black-currant sauce.

In 1996, after being nominated in the first year of the awards and for six consecutive years, D'Amato made history as the first Wisconsinite to win the James Beard Award for Best Chef: Midwest. By 2001, *Gourmet* had placed Sanford among the top fifty restaurants in America. With that, the grocery store turned eatery became Milwaukee's claim to restaurant fame.

In December 2012, Sandy and Angie sold Sanford to their longtime chef de cuisine, Justin Aprahamian, who currently runs the restaurant with the help of his wife, Sarah, much as Sandy did.

THE BARTOLOTTA RESTAURANTS

Around the time Sanford was really hitting its stride, a different Milwaukee institution was starting to take shape. It began with another ordinary Italian American family—this time at the dinner table. "According to my father, we were 100 percent Italian," said Joe Bartolotta, now president of Bartolotta Restaurants. "According to my mother, who was German, we were fifty-fifty."

Sicilian by descent, food always played a starring role in the Bartolotta household. "Every Saturday, my dad would go to the market," Joe recalled. "And he'd buy his sausage, ham, Pecorino, the ingredients to make meatballs and great Italian bread from Sciortino's." But back then, Joe had no idea that he and his brother, Paul, would end up in the restaurant industry.

Paul and Joe Bartolotta. *Courtesy of the Bartolotta Restaurants.*

From the early age of fifteen, Paul Bartolotta found himself drawn to culinary pastimes. He made pizza at Balistreri's, worked the line at the Chancery and eventually landed a job working under the guidance of John Marangelli, one of Milwaukee's best-known Italian chefs. Marangelli encouraged him to attend culinary school at Milwaukee Area Technical College. "I worked with him for more than two years," Paul remarked. "He probably influenced my palate more than anyone else."

In 1981, Paul moved to New York, where he worked with restaurateur Tony May, then owner of the Rainbow Room and founder of the Gruppo Ristoratori Italiani. With May's support, Paul traveled to Europe, where he received a seven-year education at more than a dozen restaurants in Italy and apprenticed at four three-star Michelin restaurants in France. Before returning to the United States to head up the kitchen at San Domenico NY, Paul also worked as *chef di cucina* at the two-starred San Domenico in Imola, Italy. In 1991, he took a position as chef of Spiaggia in Chicago and became managing partner with Levy Restaurants. He would eventually make his mark, earning accolades as James Beard Foundation's Best Chef: Midwest in 1994 for his work at Spiaggia and again in 2009 as Best Chef: Southwest for his namesake restaurant: Bartolotta, Ristorante di Mare, at Wynn Las Vegas.

While Paul was in Italy, Joe moved to New York, where he aspired to soak in as much as he could about the restaurant industry. "When I moved there, the light went on," Joe recalled, "because Milwaukee hadn't really evolved at that point. And New York was really developing. California had done its spa cuisine. Wolfgang Puck started to kick out some protégés, and things were really moving forward."

Hungry to learn as much as possible, Joe spent eight years in New York, working myriad front-of-the-house positions at venues including Tavern on the Green and Maxwell's Plum before returning to Milwaukee.

It was an ordinary (but very fortunate) day in 1992 when Joe, who had been working as the food and beverage director at the Hilton, stumbled on a little restaurant at 7616 West State Street in Wauwatosa that had recently closed its doors.

Excited by the prospect of opening something of his own there, he called on Paul to give him a hand. The plan was for Paul to take charge of the kitchen and Joe to head up the management. "Joe DeRosa of the Chancery put up the money for us," Joe recalled. "We owe the whole company to him, really. He's a very good man…a good restaurateur."

With DeRosa's support, the Bartolottas hired a Chicago architect to help them renovate the space. They also brought in talented Long Island chef Marc Bianchini, whom Paul had taken under his wing at San Domenico NY and who would later carve his own impression on the Milwaukee scene.

"We wanted it to be rustic, Northern Italian cooking. Milwaukee had a lot of Sicilian places but not a lot of Northern cooking," Joe explains. "And Paul had spent the bulk of his time in North and Central Italy. So when we did caprese salad, bruschetta, fried calamari, wood-fired brick oven pizza and handmade pastas, we were the first. None of it existed in Milwaukee."

On March 23, 1993, Ristorante Bartolotta was born. It is situated in a historic building built in the 1800s and boasts fifty-five seats. The space has changed very little since the restaurant first opened: the tables are arranged in the same way, the same family photos hang on the wall and the same rustic décor adorns the bar.

For three years, DeRosa and the Bartolotta brothers maintained a partnership. "He asked me to buy him out," Joe explained of DeRosa. "I didn't want to insult him by lowballing, but I didn't want to pay too much either. I wrote down a number on a piece of paper and slid it over to him. He shook his head and said, 'Nope, ain't gonna do it.'"

Instead, he slid a counter-offer across the table. And Joe learned a lesson in business: "His number was one dollar over mine," he recollects. "He just wanted to win the negotiation. And that's how we started."

Ristorante Bartolotta garnered four stars in its first—and many subsequent—reviews, received the DiRoNA Award from Distinguished Restaurants of North America and has consistently been named the best Italian restaurant in Milwaukee.

The restaurant also opened the floodgates for what would soon be a restaurant empire. Impressively, over the course of the next seventeen years, the Bartolottas would open twelve more restaurants and three catering establishments, including Lake Park Bistro (1996); Nonna Bartolotta's (1998); Mr. B's Steakhouse (1999); Harbor House (2010); Pizzeria Piccola (2003); Bacchus, a Bartolotta Restaurant (2004); Northpoint Custard (2008); Rumpus Room, a Bartolotta Gastropub (2011); Joey Gerard's, a Bartolotta Supperclub (2012); and Miss Beverly's Deluxe Barbeque (2014). They would also take over operation of Downtown Kitchen, an on-site food court in the U.S. Bank Center on Wisconsin Avenue, and break ground in 2015 on a trio of restaurants located in the Mayfair Collection, a retail, dining and nightlife destination on Milwaukee's West Side.

Along the way, these restaurants would provide a training ground for some of Milwaukee's best chefs and front-of-house personnel. They would also establish a reputation for impeccable hospitality and consistent, spot-on cuisine, laying the groundwork—and benchmarks—for many of the chef-owned restaurants that now form the bulk of Milwaukee's restaurant landscape.

The Rise of Milwaukee's Restaurant Groups

As Ristorante Bartolotta made its mark on the fine dining scene, there were others who had similar aspirations. And the 1990s gave birth to an impressive collective of restaurateurs whose foresight and vision would help to shape the picture moving forward.

While Milwaukee has never given harbor to a significant number of chain restaurants, locals in the business have met with success with forming partnerships and establishing area restaurant groups that have given a wide variety of industry professionals their start. They have also invested the needed funds to bring new concepts into a growing restaurant scene.

Partners Scott Johnson and Leslie Montemurro were two of the industry's earliest movers and shakers. "When I was in my mid-twenties, I spent the summer in Europe," said Montemurro. "I traveled all around, and just being there really inspired me to want a café. The cafés—especially the ones in Amsterdam—were just so laid-back, and they seemed like really cool places to work."

So, in the 1990s, when Montemurro met Johnson, she convinced him to take a trip around the country. "We drove around in his Toyota minivan, going everywhere and looking at coffee shops and cafés everywhere," she said. "And I spent eight months convincing him that we needed to open one."

Montemurro's wish came true. Once they returned to Milwaukee, they hatched the plan for Fuel Café, a coffee shop at 818 East Center Street in the rough-and-tumble Riverwest neighborhood. The shop, which opened in 1993, was like no other in town—it didn't open until 9:00 a.m. And yet the shop became a popular destination filled with a motley crew of chain-smoking punk rockers and neighborhood folks.

Having met with success with Fuel, the two opened their second café, Comet on Farwell Avenue, in 1995. Meanwhile, Mike Eitel launched the Nomad World Pub just blocks away on Brady Street. The three met over many beers at the Nomad and partnered to open Hi Hat Lounge in 1998, the first modern martini lounge in the city, just down the street from the Nomad. They opened the Garage adjacent to Hi Hat the following year.

Eitel opened Trocadero as a solo effort in 2001, later selling shares to Montemurro and Johnson, while the two moved their efforts south to Bay View to start Palomino in 2002. Then, in 2004, Eric Wagner joined them on the Hi Hat, Garage and Trocadero ventures. The new foursome, under the company name Diablos Rojos, opened Balzac Wine Bar together in 2005.

More brainstorming led to the concept of a grand café, and Hollander on Downer Avenue was launched in 2007. Shortly after, the team agreed to an amicable split, resulting in Eitel and Wagner keeping Trocadero and Hollander; meanwhile, Montemurro and Johnson maintained Hi Hat, the Garage and Balzac.

Over the years, Johnson and Montemurro, who now work under the moniker Mojofuco, also entered into other partnerships. In 2005, they brought on brother-sister duo Adam and Valeri Lucks to give Comet Café a refresh and, later, Honeypie Café and Palomino, as well. In 2010, they officially partnered with longtime manager Kristyn Eitel (née St. Denis) to open BelAir Cantina on the corner of Humboldt Avenue and Water Street. A little tavern called Fink's and two more BelAirs, in Wauwatosa and on Downer Avenue, were soon to follow.

When Eitel and Wagner formed the Lowlands Group, a reference to the region in Europe that inspired the company's new focus on Belgian and Dutch "grand cafés," they added a number of establishments to their portfolio, including Café Benelux in the Third Ward, Café Centraal in Bay View and Café Hollander and Café Bavaria in the village of Wauwatosa. The group, which also brews beer under the Lowlands Brewing Collaborative, with partner brewers in Belgium, was instrumental in expanding the craft beer scene in the city while capitalizing on its European ancestry.

In 2014, the group sold Trocadero Gastropub to partners David Price, Chris Tinker, Drew Duester and J.J. Kovacovich. The same year, Eitel departed from the Lowlands Group to focus his efforts on the Nomad World Pub. In 2015, he and his wife, Kristyn, opened Panga Pub & Grill in Summit, Wisconsin.

Meanwhile, Joe and Angie Sorge founded Hospitality Democracy, a company that would make its mark on Milwaukee by offering fun and varied restaurant concepts with an emphasis on accessibility.

In 2005, Swig became Milwaukee's first small-plate dining restaurant at its initial Water Street location and one of the first trendy restaurants to take a spot on the now hopping Broadway Avenue row after its move to the Third Ward in 2008. In the meantime, the Sorges would open Water Buffalo, a casual riverfront restaurant serving American favorites, followed by AJ Bombers in 2009, a burger restaurant and bar that would set the benchmark for social media promotion among Milwaukee restaurants as it created a buzz among early adopters on Twitter, Facebook and FourSquare.

In 2011, the Sorges partnered with Marcus Investments to further develop their company portfolio, adding three restaurants in Milwaukee's Third Ward: Smoke Shack, a small barbecue restaurant; Holey Moley Doughnuts & Coffee, the city's first craft doughnut shop; and Onesto, an Italian restaurant.

SURG Restaurant Group is one of the newest groups on the scene. But the group's partners, Omar Shaikh and Mike Polaski, have been around longer. Shaikh opened Carnevor in 2006, and Polaski opened both Umami Moto in Brookfield and Mi-Key's shortly before the two joined forces in 2010. "It was always our vision to create a restaurant row on Milwaukee Street," said Shaikh. "And even though we are 'big box' units, we still create things from scratch."

Attention to detail, including a pastry program established by renowned pastry chef Kurt Fogle (who departed in 2015 to take an executive chef position at Bass Bay Brewhouse in Muskego, Wisconsin) and a butchering and curing facility, are hallmarks of SURG's presence. Most of the restaurants are intimate and all are meticulously constructed, with many developed by local talent at Flux Design.

The company's presence now includes a dozen locations throughout downtown Milwaukee and the suburbs, including Carnevor, Bugsy's, Distil, Gouda's Italian Deli, two locations of Hōm Woodfired Grill, Lucid Hookah & Light Lounge, Mi-Key's, Umami Moto, the Garden and SURG on the Water, both private events venues.

Milwaukee's newest restaurant group, Black Shoe Hospitality, formed in 2014, as Dan Sidner and Chef Joe Muench, the owners of Maxie's and Blue's Egg, moved forward to open a third restaurant, Story Hill BKC. The partners decided that it was time to put a name to the projects. "The hope was to really form a group identity, create some esprit de corps among the team members of all three of the restaurants and make it easier to introduce ourselves at cocktail parties," Sidner said with a smile.

Choosing a name, Sidner admitted, wasn't easy. Many seemed too uptight or condescending; others sounded too cute or overly whimsical. The group needed something that encompassed its goals and values—the provision of delicious food, stellar hospitality and dedication to supporting local causes and organizations.

"The leading name for the better part of a year was 'Not Corporate Guys,'" said Sidner. "Then one morning, Joe was putting on his shoes—his very typical black kitchen work shoes—and it hit him: Black Shoe. Anyone who has ever worked in the hospitality industry has needed a good, solid pair of shoes in order to put in the day's work. And those shoes aren't fancy or fashionable; they're comfortable and sturdy."

The name, Black Shoe Hospitality, would ultimately reflect the goal that powers all of Muench and Sidner's restaurants: to deliver genuine hospitality that zeroes in on what a guest wants or needs and then working hard to deliver it.

These groups, along with the growing Bartolotta's empire, laid the needed groundwork for a diverse restaurant scene, giving rise to the public's appetite for the chef-driven restaurants of today.

Farm to Fork

In the past ten years, farm-to-table dining has become the norm in restaurants across the country. "Eat local" has become a buzz phrase, encouraging consumers to pay attention to the place from which their food comes.

Although states with longer growing seasons tend to take the credit for their ability to heed the call for local, Milwaukee has actually been at the forefront of the movement. And a great deal of credit for that goes to Wisconsin's agricultural prowess. According to the Wisconsin Department of Agriculture, Trade and Consumer Protection, the state is the number-one producer of cranberries, ginseng roots, whey and snap beans for processing. It's also the country's largest producer of cheese (and fourth-largest in the world), with nearly 1,200 licensed cheese makers who produce more than six hundred types, styles and varieties of cheese, nearly double that of any other state. Wisconsin ranks second in organic production and boasts a plethora of both cherry and apple orchards. And farms here harvest potatoes from sixty-three thousand acres of land, ranking the state third in potato production.

Despite the shortcomings of a relatively brief growing season, the farm-to-table movement in the area has grown by leaps and bounds. Milwaukee chefs have been able to capitalize on Wisconsin's bounty, showcasing creativity on increasingly localized seasonal menus and extending the harvest through means like preservation.

But the sea change from national to local sourcing didn't happen overnight. And in Milwaukee, it developed largely due to the influence of a few key players.

ROOTS RESTAURANT AND CELLAR

In 2003, long before area restaurants began crediting farmers on their menus, John Raymond became one of the pioneers of the Milwaukee farm-to-table movement. "The dream began when I was born," said Raymond, wistfully. "I was raised on a farm, with my hands in the dirt and from-scratch cooking all around me."

After earning his culinary degree at Waukesha County Technical College, Raymond got his start as apprentice at the Ville Du Park Country Club in Mequon before taking executive chef positions at a variety of Milwaukee restaurants, including Café Vecchio Mondo, Café Marché and Red Rock Café.

"The idea for Roots Restaurant and Cellar really began to solidify in 1996 and '97, when I started working with a local farmer," said Raymond. "The whole idea of 'farm to fork' is kind of a misnomer, because all food comes from a farm. But this stemmed from a passion. It was about growing the best, connecting with the food, harvesting it."

So, in 2002, after a stint as executive chef and general manager of Vinifera, Raymond pulled together the talents of his front-of-house manager and his dear friend and farmer Joe Schmidt, making history by opening Roots Restaurant and Cellar, the state's first chef- and farmer-owned restaurant, in the Brewer's Hill neighborhood at 1818 North Hubbard Street.

The restaurant, which originally farmed about one and a half acres at Cedar Creek Farm in Cedarburg, north of Milwaukee, later moving to a plot at the Family Farm in nearby Grafton, focused its energy on seasonal, regional American fare built on the notion that fresh and local were paramount. "When we opened, I had a lot of people saying that it wouldn't work," Raymond recalled. "And there were definitely challenges. Farmers didn't have the means to deliver produce to us, so we were picking it up from them."

Another big obstacle was dealing with copious amounts of produce during the peak season, as well as processing it in ways that it could supply the restaurant year round. "Some weeks, we'd have seven hundred pounds of tomatoes to process," he remembered. "But what better thing is there to have than summer tomato soup in the winter? And to be able to call it local?"

So, when the restaurant faced one hundred pounds of summer squash and thirty pounds of carrots, along with nonstop salad greens, cardoons and tomatillos, the staff would work countless hours, pickling, processing, vacuum sealing and dehydrating. "The stockpots were never off the stove,"

Raymond said. "The freezer was never empty. And there was no #10 can to be found in the restaurant."

But the efforts were worth it, said Raymond, for whom the concept was as much about quality cuisine as supporting the local agricultural industry. "I loved regional American cuisine," he said, "and I used as much as I could from all coasts. All of our fish was flown in from Hawaii every other day or from Pacific Seafood. Scallops came in from Viking Village in New Jersey. Game came from Wisconsin, Colorado, Minnesota. Grains were artisan from South Carolina, milled the right way—on grindstones, with fair pay for the farmers."

In addition to the crops Schmidt grew, Raymond also sourced actively from area farmers and foragers. At Roots' peak, Raymond estimates that he had a network of around twenty-seven local producers. "There was a farmer who brought me cases of quince from Burlington," he recalled. "He'd sell to Frontera Grill in Chicago and to Sanford. But we had a special relationship because I'd take all of his seconds for processing. And there was the papaw farmer from Racine and a little old lady who would pop up into my driveway and ask me if I wanted flats of red currants. I'd never ask her the price; I'd just say yes. That's just the sort of relationships I had with farmers and producers."

Being ahead of the curve presented challenges, too. "Consumers were hesitant," said Raymond. "And we were considered to be an 'organic' restaurant for far too long. We had to break down walls there because it scared people."

But the restaurant gained a loyal following for its fresh, seasonal cuisine and inventive vegetarian and vegan entrées. And as the local food movement grew and organic produce became available on the shelves of local grocery stores, the message of Roots began to resonate.

In 2008, as the economy turned south, Raymond found himself needing to focus more on the business end of the restaurant, so he handed over the reins in the kitchen to then sous chef Paul Zerkel, who subsequently passed the torch to Daniel Jacobs in 2012. "Paul would visit the farm and say, 'I want that lamb,'" Raymond recalled. "And we'd bring it in. We'd get in whole pigs, half pigs. Our fish was butchered in house, and nothing went to waste. We'd cure the intestines with salt to make our own sausages. We'd cure and smoke hams and corn beef brisket. We did everything we could possibly do in house."

Before its closing in late 2012, Roots would enjoy eight consecutive years on the "Top 30" restaurants list in the *Milwaukee Journal-Sentinel*, as well as features in *Bon Appétit, Cooking Light, Organic Living, National Geographic*

Traveler and *Gourmet*. In 2011, it earned honors as highest-rated restaurant in Milwaukee by Zagat. Roots would also build a legacy, paving the way for a new generation of restaurants whose focus on fresh, local, seasonal cuisine would become the norm in the Cream City.

BRAISE

Chef Dave Swanson of Braise. *Photo by Joe Laedtke.*

Ask anyone about farm-to-table dining in Milwaukee, and Dave Swanson's name is certain to come up. And his restaurant, Braise, is sure to follow shortly behind. But Swanson's legacy is about more than being a restaurateur. It's about helping to change the way the local food system operates.

Swanson, who grew up in Illinois and trained at Kendall College in Evanston, said that he came by the notion of local, regionally based cooking fairly naturally. "My dad had a garden, [and] my mom always cooked from scratch," he said. "I'd go to my grandmother's house, and she'd make a rhubarb tart for us as a snack. So it was kind of always part of my fiber."

As a teenager, Swanson worked as a dishwasher. During culinary school, he interned at renowned Le Titi de Paris, studying under Pierre Pollin, and went on to work at Commander's Palace in New Orleans, as well as the famed Le Francais in Wheeling, Illinois.

Swanson met Chef Sanford D'Amato when he participated in a collaborative dinner at Le Francais. "I told him what I wanted to do," said Swanson. "I was burned out on Chicago and wanted to get back to a more earnest and honest lifestyle. Ideally, I wanted to work at a seasonal New American place; somewhere that was more high profile."

D'Amato offered Swanson a position at Sanford, where he worked his way up from sous chef to chef de cuisine. During his six years there, he developed the cooking style and philosophy that would later define his work at Braise. "One of the things that solidified the Braise journey was my experience at Commander's Palace," he recalled. "In New Orleans, it was about ingredients raised, grown and produced there…crab, creole tomatoes, creole mustard, Tabasco sauce. Seeing the pride in what they produce. At Le Francais, we sourced many of our ingredients from Wisconsin. And we did the same at Sanford. But I always had it in the back of my head that we could do it on a larger level."

While at Sanford, Swanson watched as Roots Restaurant and Cellar was coming into fruition and seeing success with sourcing more local products. He researched East Coast food hubs that created economies for restaurants and farmers. He got involved with Slow Food Southeast Wisconsin. And he began tweaking a business plan he'd started while living in New Orleans, a plan that detailed a restaurant and teaching facility that relied on locally sourced products as its foundation.

In 2004, Swanson left Sanford and informally launched the Braise on the Go Traveling Culinary School, which hosted pop-up dinners at area farms. As he got to know more and more farmers, he also got to know more about roadblocks they faced distributing to local restaurants. And he began to toy with the idea of a distribution system.

By 2007, with the help of a $35,000 grant from Buy Local Buy Wisconsin and $15,000 from the Brico Fund, Swanson was ready to roll out the plan for his Restaurant Supported Agriculture (RSA) program, a mechanism by which he'd facilitate distribution between Wisconsin farmers and local chefs and restaurateurs through collective buying. A project that began with one farm and four founding restaurant members now supports a full warehouse of produce from more than eighty farmers, supplying to twenty-five area restaurants per week.

But its start was rocky. "Wisconsin experienced massive flooding that year," recalled Swanson. "The timing couldn't have been worse. But we improvised by working with a lot of commodity products like onions and carrots and began to make inroads with what we were trying to do."

The concept, which was based on research Swanson collected regarding food hubs and distribution programs around the United States, created an economy meant to work for both small farms and restaurants. "I started by interviewing restaurants about what they needed," said Swanson. "If Peter Sandroni [of La Merenda] wanted twenty pounds of carrots a week, how much would we need to order? I'd pull the numbers together and contract with the farm to grow eight hundred pounds of carrots."

According to Swanson, the RSA saw sales of $6,000 in its first year, admittedly a slow start for a program he hoped to grow to sustain the needs of as many restaurants as possible. But with farms struggling—and restaurants looking for ways to bring in more produce—his determination increased.

Sometimes Swanson picked up deliveries himself. Eventually, he collaborated with area businesses like Outpost Natural Food Cooperative, and by and by, the process became more efficient. Swanson established a warehouse space in Bay View, allowing him to bring in a larger volume of produce. He also began to increase the number of restaurants he served.

Along the way, Swanson realized that broadening his services to include consumers was a logical move. "In my research, when I looked at breaking down cattle, I knew that places could use chuck or ground beef, but it was hard to sell restaurants on the idea of buying one tenderloin. It was a weekend special at best. So we started a home delivery service, beginning with five families and growing to more than one hundred."

For three years, Swanson poured his energy into the RSA and a home delivery program he developed as a subset of the business. But by 2010, he had begun looking in earnest for a space to house the restaurant and culinary school, eventually deciding on a building in Walker's Point that had previously housed a French bistro and a cocktail lounge.

"Since 2001, I spent a lot of time looking at spaces, popping in on places that went up for sale," Swanson said. "Ultimately, it was the footprint of this building that really spoke to me. We knew we had infrastructure for a rooftop garden, an upstairs event space and a teaching kitchen."

When it came to the cuisine, Swanson said he wanted to get back to basics. "Obviously, working in French restaurants with thirty cooks, you can do really intricate plating. But I wanted to showcase more elevated bistro food," he said. "Something simple, straightforward, that pays homage to the ingredients and what the farmers do."

Braise Restaurant opened in December 2011. The culinary school launched in the fall of the following year. And in December 2013, the restaurant finished the installment of a rooftop garden and patio. Beginning that same year, Swanson was a semifinalist for the James Beard Best Chef: Midwest award for three years running.

House-made cheese with mushroom salad at Braise. *Photo by Joe Laedtke.*

But Swanson said that Braise has never been his vanity project. In fact, he hopes to one day open a restaurant that more intimately captures his own style. "Seeing these systems take shape has been gratifying," Swanson admitted. "Braise is a teaching kitchen where people learn how to cook with these fresh ingredients. And it is a business built around local food and ways to really support that, how to build efficiencies with it. But honestly, this project has never really been about me. This is about the food and the farmers."

La Merenda

When Peter Sandroni opened La Merenda—an international tapas restaurant focused on sourcing as much local, seasonal produce as possible—he did so very deliberately. "I wasn't throwing things at the wall, seeing what would stick," he said. "I'd purposely been exposed to all sorts of cuisines—Hispanic, Central American, Asian, French, Filipino—and at the time even restaurants in Chicago weren't tackling the international idea."

Sandroni—who, like Dave Swanson of Braise, trained at Kendall College—said that it was his work for Jennifer Aranas at Rambutan in

Chef Peter Sandroni of La Merenda and Engine Company No. 3. *Photo by Joe Laedtke.*

Chicago that turned him on to the idea of international tapas. "She said to me, 'You're so good at all of these cuisines, you should put together an international restaurant.'"

Her words stuck. Five years later, during a stint working at Eagan's on Water in Milwaukee, Sandroni began building a business plan. "I had taken what she said to heart," he recalled. "I wanted to open a breakfast place, but as I thought more about it, I thought the international tapas idea would be fun."

Milwaukeeans were largely familiar with the idea of tapas, thanks to restaurants like Don Quixote, a restaurant that served Spanish tapas for more than a decade before closing in 2008. So Sandroni felt sure that he could make the concept work. And he felt strongly that sourcing locally should be part of the concept. "I'd worked at a spot in Atlanta where there was a farmers' market adjacent to the restaurant. I saw the value of using items that had been picked in the last day or two. It was simple, but I loved it. And I wanted to employ more of it."

So, Sandroni made it part of his business plan. In 2006, Sandroni opened La Merenda in an old woodworking shop on a dead-end street in Walker's Point. At the time, the area had only one truly notable restaurant: Peggy

Magister's Crazy Water, a pricey (by local standards) bistro with a quietly loyal clientele. But Sandroni held firm, convinced that La Merenda could make a splash in the not-yet-discovered neighborhood.

He knew that many restaurants, including Rambutan, had been sourcing ingredients from Wisconsin farms for years, so he made it a point to begin connecting with them, along with other smaller farms that didn't have the infrastructure to deliver to Chicago.

In the meantime, Sandroni also connected with Dave Swanson, who was just getting started with his restaurant-supported agriculture program and signed on as one of his first customers. The relationships grew from there. Soon, Sandroni was connected to a statewide network of vendors that supplied not only produce but also meat and dairy products. He was also sourcing more local products than almost any restaurant in the city.

The first few years were rough, Sandroni admitted. He'd opened just before the economy took a downturn in 2008, and business was slow to pick up. But the lure of delicious international fare at a relatively affordable price seemed enough to launch La Merenda into customers' favor. These days, it's difficult to find a seat there, particularly on weekends, and reservations are highly recommended.

The success of La Merenda, as well as the desire to keep pushing himself creatively, inspired Sandroni to make a move in 2014, when he opened another farm-to-table spot in an old firehouse just down the street from La Merenda. He said that the idea for Engine Company No. 3 was always percolating. "Ever since I worked at the Bongo Room in Chicago, I've wanted to do breakfast. And when the property became available, and I knew we had to move on it. It was really important that the two restaurants be close to one another. And we wouldn't find anything closer. So we took advantage of that."

And while some restaurants might see breakfast as inferior to dinner, with lower margins and less overall appeal, Sandroni feels strongly about it. "It's a different time of day," he said, "and we're taking dinner principles and trying to apply them at breakfast, the way the menu is designed for food and drinks, as well as the service we provide. There are some people who take breakfast very seriously in this town, and we want to tap into that."

For Sandroni, it's also about continuing to support local farmers and producers. "Buying locally is about economic impact, flavor, nutritional value, freshness," he said. "But actually, one of the biggest reasons I do it now is relationships. It's something Milwaukeeans do very well. People talk with one another. It just happens here. And the relationships we create with farmers are great. Why wouldn't I want to continue to buy spinach from someone I know? I can see the impact I have on them, and they see the impact they have on me. It's mutual."

That mutual benefit includes contracting with area farmers to buy a certain allotment of product in a given year. "Turtle Creek is a good example," he said. "Janet Gamble from Turtle Creek Gardens approached me about the idea of making tomato puree for the bloody marys at Engine Company. She planted two thousand tomato plants, and we paid her to make the puree for our bloody marys. We went through it all in less than four months. Now we're talking about how to quadruple that to give us a year-round supply."

Today, Sandroni's restaurants are surrounded by a plethora of popular eateries, including Dave Swanson's Braise, Thomas Hauck's c. 1880, Jonathon Manyo's Morel and Peggy Magister's AP Bar and Kitchen. The restaurants are within blocks of some of the Cream City's most acclaimed artisanal producers, among them cheese maker Clock Shadow Creamery, Purple Door Ice Cream, Anodyne Coffee Roasting Company, Milwaukee Brewing Company and both Central Standard and Great Lakes Distilleries. The city is also filled with restaurants that maintain varying commitments to local sourcing. It began as a national trend but has become best practice for Milwaukee chefs who have grown to recognize—and capitalize on—the agricultural bounty of the state in which they work.

Urban Producers

Wisconsin's agricultural history is long and storied. And our ability to produce record-breaking amounts of food in a midwestern growing season is impressive.

In 2014, the total net farm income in Wisconsin reached an all-time high of more than $4 billion. And despite a decline in both farms and farmland being utilized in the state, Wisconsin remains among the top-ten agricultural states in number of farms and agricultural sales. In fact, according to data from the U.S. Department of Agriculture, the state had 69,756 farms covering nearly 14.6 million acres in 2012.

The abundance of food produced in the state of Wisconsin makes Milwaukee an excellent place for restaurants to thrive. Many chefs in the city value their personal relationships with farmers and foragers, and they make special efforts to visit the farms and pick up produce for their restaurants. Other chefs collaborate on deliveries or purchase food from area farmers' markets. For those who would prefer a more traditional delivery model, distribution networks like Braise RSA have filled the gap.

But there's another part of the local food puzzle that's growing rapidly: urban farming. Since Growing Power established its farm on the northwest side of Milwaukee in 1993, others have followed suit. Greenhouses are popping up in area warehouses and vacant lots. Neighborhoods are seizing formerly unused spaces to start community gardens. And urban farmers are marketing themselves to chefs as a mechanism for gaining even better access to local produce.

In addition to overall support for the creation of jobs and urban greenspace, numerous initiatives have bolstered the growth of the urban farming movement. The University of Wisconsin Extension recently launched its MicroFarming Program, an initiative that researches the economic viability and social capital of urban agriculture while empowering small-scale farmers in the region. The program teaches urban farmers how to use sustainable methods to increase their food production while cultivating buyer relationships with partnered Milwaukee restaurants, markets and food co-ops.

Meanwhile, Mayor Tom Barrett and the City of Milwaukee launched Home Gr/own, an initiative that aims to pull together food- and farming-related programs to transform problems like unemployment, foreclosures and urban decay into fertile ground for a good food economy. In exchange for training, business development assistance and improvement of urban food infrastructure, the city hopes to encourage urban producers to sell their goods directly through farmers' markets, restaurants and grocers. The goals of the program include the implementation of new healthy food access and greenspace developments, making it easier to grow and distribute healthy food, and supporting new urban farms and healthy food retailers and wholesalers. Through the program, the city has supported 177 community gardens on city land and has given grants to sustainable farming operations, such as Growing Power.

GROWING POWER

The story of Will Allen and Growing Power is ubiquitous in the development of urban farming in the United States. It was launched in 1993, when Allen purchased an abandoned garden center with three acres of land on Milwaukee's northwest side. The retired professional basketball player was raised on a farm, and once his career came to a close, he turned to cultivating produce on his wife's family farm. The purchased lot was intended to be a site where he could sell the produce he'd grown. But when he found out that the small property was the last tract in the city of Milwaukee still zoned for agriculture, he was inspired to grow food there.

Allen soon adopted the role of mentor, as urban youth began to take an interest in his project and in learning how to grow food. He became an innovator in methods of composting, vermicomposting (composting with the help of worms) and aquaponics, practices that result in remarkable yields of food, even in a very small area. And what began as a small business became a community-building educational facility that would influence many other urban farms in the years to come.

Today, Growing Power produces more than two hundred crops on more than three hundred acres of land. Using vermicomposting bins and waste digesters, the organization composts more than 40 million pounds of refuse annually. And its impact on the community, as well as the nation, has been immeasurable.

The organization has spearheaded numerous projects, including assisting organizations with garden projects, launching regional training centers to aid in its mission to build sustainable food systems, helping to supply local fresh food to public school lunch programs and providing countless educational opportunities and programming for youth and aspiring urban farmers. "It takes a long time to grow a sustainable urban farmer," said Allen. "As I travel around the country and around the world, I meet all sorts of young people who want to be farmers, who like the idea of doing what I do. But they have no idea how to do it or how hard it is to make a living doing it. The infrastructure and costs involved are huge."

Aquaponics is one of the biggest developments that's taking off in Milwaukee, said Allen. The model is sustainable and can be a catalyst for job creation and economic development in urban areas. The flexibility is part of its appeal, as an aquaponics facility can be built in a greenhouse, warehouse or even in a pole barn. Growing Power has even brought the model into elementary and high schools, installing tanks in thirty-seven schools in the metro-Milwaukee area. "Through our program, we're teaching these young grade school and high school kids about biology and the sciences," he said. "It leads to them digging deeper and learning more. It's one of the best ways to educate kids today—to have them work on something hands-on that piques their interest."

Growing Power has also tackled obstacles related to bringing fresh, nourishing food to urban areas. A Farm-to-City Market Basket program distributes more than three hundred baskets of fresh food to residents in low-income areas of Milwaukee at a subsidized rate. The organization also operates a community-supported agriculture (CSA) program, as well as heading up the Rainbow Farmers Cooperative, a network of small family farmers in Wisconsin, Illinois, Michigan and Iowa.

In July 2012, Growing Power opened a café and market in Milwaukee's Harambee neighborhood, offering fresh produce, some groceries and a menu of soups, sandwiches, salads and pastries at affordable prices. It was a welcome addition to a neighborhood without many options for fresh local food. In addition to prepared items, the café also offers vegetables from Growing Power, such as eggplant, peppers and tomatoes, along with fruit from other sources. The shelves are stocked with mostly organic products, including cereal, granola, whole-grain pasta and gluten-free flour.

Today, more than 90 percent of the food that enters the market from urban farms comes from Growing Power, a significant amount of which is sold to area restaurants. In addition to its own café, Growing Power supplies fresh produce to more than a dozen Milwaukee-area restaurants, including Honeypie, Distil, Meritage and Sanford, as well as numerous venues in the Potawatomi Hotel & Casino. Lakefront Brewery buys the full crop of fileted perch produced at Growing Power's facility to serve at its weekly Friday fish fry. And thanks to a partnership with Sysco, the organization distributes hundreds of cases of salad mix to additional restaurants, grocery stores and area institutions, including Milwaukee Public Schools.

"The public has demanded locally grown food," said Allen, "and everybody has to be at the table if we really want to get good local, healthy food into places where people really shop. One of the biggest challenges we face is how to get produce into big-box stores and have it labeled so that people can find it easily."

Urban food production has become a calling for Allen, who has become the international face of urban agriculture and an influential voice on the subject of food policy. *TIME* magazine named him one of the World's Most Influential People in 2010, and Allen won a $500,000 MacArthur Foundation "Genius Grant" in 2008.

In 2014, Allen wrote *The Good Food Revolution: Growing Healthy Food, People and Communities* (Gotham Books). It's the story of his personal journey, the lives he has touched and a grass-roots movement that is changing the way our nation eats. "My father taught me that the fate of a seed can be predicted by the health of the soil where it takes root," wrote Allen. "This is true of summer crops. It can be true, in another sense, of people. We all need a healthy environment and a community that lets us fulfill our potential."

CLOCK SHADOW CREAMERY

Milwaukee native Bob Wills has become something of a legend in the cheese making world. He hadn't given any thought to the idea of devoting his life to cheese before marrying into a cheese making family at the age of thirty-two. But things change.

In 1989, he purchased Cedar Grove Cheese in Plain, Wisconsin, a cheese factory that he transformed into a green facility featuring recycling and energy reduction programs, as well as a "Living Machine," which uses natural microbes and hydroponic for washwater treatment, creating clean water that is then discharged into a nearby creek.

During his more than twenty-five-year career, Wills has mentored many up-and-coming cheese makers including Mike Gingrich of Uplands Cheese and Al Bekkum of Nordic Creamery. And in 2012, he decided to contribute his influence in cheese making to the Milwaukee food scene.

Bob Wills of Clock Shadow Creamery. *Photo by Joe Laedtke.*

Named for the nearby Allen-Bradley Clock Tower, Milwaukee's first cheese factory, Clock Shadow Creamery, was established to cultivate interest in urban cheese making while providing a fresh local product to urban residents and businesses.

To bring the project to fruition, Wills partnered with Milwaukee developer Juli Kaufmann to lease the first floor of a new $7.2 million, four-story green structure at 138 West Bruce Street. The building, now known as the Clock Shadow Building, was designed to be energy efficient and carbon neutral. It incorporates a rooftop garden and beehives, on-site food composting, water reuse and geothermal components, as well as off-site wind turbines.

"Everybody has been promoting local food, but some of the definitions of 'local' that people are using are pretty lax," Wills remarked. "But really, the point of local is to be able to target the needs and tastes of consumers in a particular location. So I said, let's take the opportunity to focus on where the real advantage is in local products—and that's on fresh, customized products."

In an effort to support farmers on the urban fringe, who are under constant pressure to sell their land to developers, products made at the creamery are produced from rBGH-free milk procured from nearby suburban family dairy farms. A recent partnership with the Milwaukee County Zoo farm also provides an urban source of fresh milk for cheese making.

The creamery began production with one of Wills's personal favorites: quark. A European fresh cheese with a mild flavor and soft texture, quark is made by warming soured milk to denature its proteins and then straining it until it reaches the desired creamy consistency. The creamery also produces fresh cheese curds, ricotta, cheddar and Mexican-style cheeses, like *queso Menonita* and *queso blanco*. It produces Bon Bree cheese with milk from the Williams family farm in Waukesha, as well as LaBelle, a Wisconsin original cheese made with milk from Koepke Farms in Oconomowoc. In 2014, the creamery also began making fresh chevre, goat cheddar, curds and Capriko, a mild cheese made from both cow's and goat's milk with a similar consistency to cheddar.

Since 2012, the creamery has played host to Martha Davis Kipcak of Mighty Fine Foods LLC, who uses the facility to make Martha's Pimento Cheese, a first-prize winner in the 2013 American Cheese Society competition.

In addition to cheese production, the creamery contributes to the community by way of education. Tours are available both to the public and to local schools like the Milwaukee Institute for Art and Design. The creamery regularly hosts classes on cheese making, sanitation and small-scale food manufacturing for Milwaukee Area Technical College, which has partnered with FaB Wisconsin, a consortium of food and beverage manufacturers, to develop the Food Maker School and Center of Excellence at 816 West National Avenue. The facility will provide space for the technical college to offer instructional technical food programs, a pilot-scale sauce production line with co-pack capacity and laboratories for product development, food analysis and microbiology testing.

The creamery sells cheeses at the factory and distributes to area retail outlets and restaurants. "Braise, La Merenda and the Iron Horse are among those who have been consistent supporters from day one," said Wills. "Newer restaurants like Ale Asylum Riverhouse have also begun to incorporate quark and a new non-melt cheese into their menus."

In addition to making an appearance at area restaurants, Clock Shadow products like quark can be found in certain varieties of Purple Door Ice Cream, a Walker's Point business that started out leasing space from the creamery before building a shop down the street.

Moving forward, the creamery hopes to establish additional local collaborations. Conversations have begun with local distilleries about a whey-based vodka and perhaps a milk-based spirit. Partnership opportunities are also being explored with area breweries, local food processors and companies like Indulgence Chocolatiers, a chocolate shop and production facility just blocks away. "The enthusiastic reception of our products and the chance to work with the local community to develop new ones has been a delight," said Wills. "The possibilities seem endless."

Sugar Bee Farm

In nature, the life of a mushroom begins with a single spore. Ousted from its home nestled in the cap of its mature mother, the spore detaches, drifting through the air until it unites with other compatible spores, forming a new mycelium, the plant body of a mushroom. From there, the mycelium feeds off dry dead carbon—usually leaves or wood—producing a new fruiting body that rises above the earth and begins the cycle all over again.

"Each mushroom variety has its own delicate character," said farmer Sebastian Zoric Martinez of Sugar Bee Farm on Milwaukee's South Side. "Simply sautéed in butter, you experience a slightly different texture and flavor with each one—flavors that range from nutty to buttery to earthy."

The mushrooms are cultivated in plastic bags filled with inoculated straw and mushroom spores. The mushroom bags spend about two weeks in a room where the mycelium begins to digest the straw and absorb nutrients for growth. From there, they are moved to a climate-controlled fruiting room, which is designed to trigger the mycelium to reproduce. The entire process takes four to six weeks.

Zoric Martinez, who was born in Santa Fe, New Mexico, spent the bulk of his childhood in Germany. He completed high school in Maine, after which he attended Carthage College in Kenosha, earning a degree in German cultural studies. From there, he moved on to Baltimore before returning to Maine to work as a behavioral technician at a residential care facility. There he learned the art of using agriculture as a tool to motivate and inspire troubled children.

Here in Wisconsin, he moved on to positions at Growing Power in Milwaukee and Buddha Baby Farm in River Hills (now in Cedarburg). There he grew a variety of seasonal vegetables for restaurants, along with indoor-grown microgreens in the winter. "It was the happiest I've ever been," said Martinez. "I was working so hard, but it didn't feel like work. The simplicity of raising food was so moving."

By 2013, he had connected with Sarah Wisniewski and Dave Grow, then owners of Sugar Bee Farm. After interning there, Zoric Martinez became part owner in 2014 and took over full operation of the farm in spring of 2015. "It was challenging," he said. "Most of the revenue from the farm was being used to pay back the loans used to start the business."

But Martinez felt strongly that the business had good bones and could be expanded to the extent that it would be self-sustaining. He also felt inspired by the notion of supplying the community with a high-quality product at a competitive price. "I'm fortunate that my wife has a great job," he said. "It affords me the luxury of not having to rely on the income from the farm, and it gives me time to build the business to the point where it can really take off."

Everything about Sugar Bee Farm is based on a philosophy of locality. The straw in which the mushrooms grow comes from Schuett Farms in Mukwonago. Meanwhile, spores are sourced from Joe Krawczyk and Mary Ellen Kozak of Field & Forest in Peshtigo, Wisconsin.

Sugar Bee Farm sells its mushrooms wholesale to Outpost Natural Food Cooperative, as well as through area farmers' markets, including the Milwaukee County Winter Market, the Tosa Farmers' Market and the Green Corridor Sixth Street Farmers' Market. But sales to restaurants currently compose as much as 80 percent of the farm's business. Martinez currently works with sixteen restaurants on a weekly basis, such as Odd Duck, Goodkind, Braise Restaurant and RSA and Black Shoe Hospitality.

"It's enticing to pursue other markets, and some have encouraged us to go that way, but I really feel that there's enough demand here in Milwaukee," said Martinez. "For me, it's ideal to really stay local, provide for my community and keep the quality as high—and the product as fresh—as possible."

WALNUT WAY

When Sharon Adams moved away from the Lindsay Heights neighborhood in 1968, it was a close-knit and prosperous community. When she returned in 1997, she found that her old home had vastly changed. Residents were in despair. Prostitution, drugs and crime were rampant. Boarded-up homes were the norm. And police advised anyone venturing near to "stay out of the neighborhood…it's too dangerous."

In 1998, Adams, her husband, Larry, and other residents founded the Walnut Way Conservation Corporation. The mission of the organization was to foster neighborhood well-being through community organizing, property restoration and economic development.

In little more than ten years, the Walnut Way Conservation Corporation and community members have successfully reclaimed the neighborhood, driven out crime, restored century-old homes, helped to construct new owner-occupied homes and created a caring neighborhood once again. They have also constructed an environmental campus that produces locally grown food on unused inner-city property.

Larry took the lead in repurposing fourteen vacant lots and blighted land into vegetable gardens, an apiary (which produces the only honey in central-city Milwaukee, as well as wax and bee pollen) and fruit orchards on which local youth grow and harvest 3,500 pounds of heirloom vegetables, herbs, peaches and pears annually. Harvests are sold to retail venues, including the Fondy Farmers' Market, Riverwest Co-Op and Galst Grocery Store, as well as restaurants like La Merenda.

Other types of produce, including specialty peppers and tomatoes, have been marketed to local food businesses, including the Salsa Lady and Man's Best Friend hot sauce company. In addition to providing revenue for the neighborhood, the environmental campus provides both social and educational resources for area adults and youth, resulting in backyard gardens and more than forty rain gardens being installed across the neighborhood. In 2014, a hoop house was built to extend the neighborhood's growing season. Plans for additional orchard crops—including peaches, pears and cherries—are in the works, as is an expansion of the produce selection, including a variety of mushrooms.

In 2015, Walnut Way broke ground on its most recent project, converting a nearly century-old building into a self-sustaining healthy food hub. The Innovations and Wellness Commons will include a pop-up Outpost Natural Food Coop grocery store, a juice bar, a commercial kitchen and administrative offices. The Commons will produce up to fifty new jobs for area residents, and the Juice Kitchen will source produce from the Walnut Way production gardens, feeding additional money back into the neighborhood economy.

The second phase of the project will include new construction to house a small grocery store (potentially run by Outpost) along with a much-needed facility focused on providing nutrition and wellness programming for the neighborhood.

CENTRAL GREENS

The former Story Hill Gardens Nursery site at Fifty-first and Bluemound was originally slated to become condominiums. But a turn in the housing market made real estate developers Sheila Firari, Mike Myers and Lance and Kathy DornBrook backtrack on their initial plans. After a conversation with the local alderman unearthed the notion that the site had potential to become an urban farm, the developers started thinking.

They took advantage of the expertise of the DornBrooks' son, Bowen, a biology major whose keen interest in horticulture, aquaculture and hydroponics developed while volunteering at Will Allen's Growing Power and Sweetwater Organics—both urban farms using aquaponic practices to produce fish and vegetables. Lance and Bowen spent nearly a year touring aquaponics farms in the Midwest and elsewhere, creating a system that pulled together the best practices from the University of the Virgin Islands, Alberta Aquaponics in Canada, Friendly Aquaponics in Hawaii and KP Simply Fresh in North Freedom, Wisconsin.

Today, the Central Greens facility harbors 1,200-gallon tanks that house an ecosystem that produces two hundred pounds of market-ready tilapia every three weeks. Fish waste becomes the natural fertilizer that feeds twelve thousand plants growing on floats in the tanks. The plants, in turn, filter the water, keeping the fish healthy.

Central Greens maintains a sustainable ecosystem in just 30 percent of the space typically used for a traditional farm. Its one-acre facility uses no chemical fertilizers, and the aquaponics system greatly reduces water costs and creates zero runoff. In addition, the farm is able to provide the community with highly nutritious, affordable and locally grown greens and fish year round.

Although 90 percent of Central Greens business is composed of sales to local retail outlets, it also distributes a number of products to area restaurants. Venues like the Black Shoe Hospitality restaurants, Mia Famiglia, Balistreri's Bluemound Inn and Café 1505 source naturally grown tilapia, as well as fifteen varieties of microgreens, sunflower, pea shoots and fresh basil.

According to Bowen DornBrook, the thriving business, which established in 2013, still has room for growth, with capacity to double its production at its current location. Over the next few years, the team expects to expand the business through national consulting on similar projects across the country.

Spring salad of salt roasted beets, shaved raw beets, feta, watercress, orange and beet syrup at Hinterland Erie Street Gastropub. *Photo by Joe Laedtke.*

Seared scallops with baby bok choy, carrot miso and peanut bergamot granola at Hinterland Erie Street Gastropub. *Photo by Joe Laedtke.*

Rotisserie lamb with vegetables at Goodkind. *Photo by Joe Laedtke.*

Parsley crusted halibut with whole grain mustard sauce, sautéed spinach and frico caldo at Crazy Water. *Photo by Joe Laedtke.*

Above: Halibut
"cioppino" with tomato
water, baharat and
fennel three ways
(pickled, roasted and
raw) at c. 1880. *Photo by
Kevin J. Miyazaki.*

Right: English pea soup
with curry, mussels and
vanilla at c. 1880. *Photo by
Kevin J. Miyazaki.*

A quiet night outside c. 1880. *Photo by Kevin J. Miyazaki.*

Foie gras with blood orange, marjoram and brioche at c. 1880. *Photo by Kevin J. Miyazaki.*

Wolf Peach dish featuring smoked Rushing Waters trout, hydroponic frisee, deep-fried baguette, watermelon radish, raw honeycomb and coal-roasted lemon purée. *Photo by Joe Laedtke.*

Cured and seared wild salmon with candied radish, pumpernickel and sorrel horseradish emulsion at Sanford Restaurant. *Photo by Joe Laedtke.*

Citrus seared striped bass on grilled corn risotto cake with pickled purslane and purslane broth at Sanford Restaurant. *Photo by Joe Laedtke.*

Fermented aged rib-eye with oak-pickled Sungold, soy-cured ramps, black garlic and dried peach preserves at Ardent. *Photo by Joe Laedtke.*

Karl Ratzsch's Restaurant. *Photo by Joe Laedtke.*

Frank Jakubczak of Milwaukee's European Homemade Sausage Shop. *Photo by Joe Laedtke.*

Urtain, a traditional Basque breakfast, at Engine Company No. 3. Includes a four-ounce sirloin, chorizo, two eggs cooked Spanish style and truffle French fries. *Photo by Joe Laedtke.*

Cubano sandwich and empanada at Cubanitas. *Photo by Joe Laedtke.*

Oppoosite, top: Engine Company No. 3's bloody mary with chaser. *Photo by Joe Laedtke.*

Opposite, bottom: Turtle French toast made with cocoa French toast batter and topped with chocolate syrup, caramel sauce and candied pecans at Engine Company No. 3. *Photo by Joe Laedtke.*

Pork with gnocchi and red cabbage from Riverside Theater. *Photo by Joe Laedtke.*

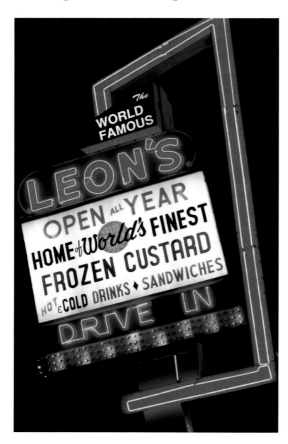

Leon's Frozen Custard, a Milwaukee fixture since 1942. *Photo by Joe Laedtke.*

Ice cream from Purple Door Ice Cream. *Photo by Joe Laedtke.*

Milwaukee Public Market. *Photo by Joe Laedtke.*

Urban beekeeping is prevalent in Milwaukee. Hives are maintained at Growing Power, Clock Shadow Creamery and even on the roof of the Pfister Hotel. *Photo by Joe Laedtke.*

Right: A beehive and a bird's-eye view from atop the Clock Shadow Creamery. *Photo by Joe Laedtke.*

Below: Rainbow carrots from area farmers' markets regularly appear on local restaurant menus. *Photo by Joe Laedtke.*

Kohlrabi is one of many vegetables grown and distributed by farmers through Braise RSA. *Photo by Joe Laedtke.*

The Milwaukee lakeshore at night. *Photo by Joe Laedtke.*

Fresh chevre from Clock Shadow Creamery. *Photo by Joe Laedtke.*

Clock Shadow Creamery. *Photo by Joe Laedtke.*

Morel Restaurant in Walker's Point. *Photo by Joe Laedtke.*

Braise Restaurant. *Photo by Joe Laedtke.*

Big City Greens

An East Side company owned by Bryan de Stefanis and his fiancée, Deborah Diaz, Big City Greens is one of the newest agricultural projects to hit the Milwaukee market. The facility, which opened in the spring of 2015, produces more than ten varieties of microgreens—including broccoli, pea, wasabi, radish, mustard, popcorn, amaranth and sunflower shoots—along with both a mild and spicy microgreen mix. The warehouse space, equipped with fans, grow-lights and skylights, also produces a variety of herbs and starter plants for De Stefanis's hobby farm in Wittenberg, Wisconsin, where he plans to cultivate heirloom vegetables to bring to market through a community supported agriculture program.

Crops on the off-site farm will be grown using organic methods, with land crops being watered by a two-acre spring-fed fish pond on the property, eliminating the need for commercial fertilizers. Meanwhile, on-site vermicomposting at the East Side facility provides rich soil for plantings while assisting in eliminating virtually all business waste.

De Stefanis, who grew up in the surrounding area, said that he's been growing vegetables his entire life. He started out helping his grandfather in the garden and moved on to begin his own landscaping company. After spending ten years operating an organic farm in the Napa Valley, De Stefanis moved back to Milwaukee.

In recent years, microgreens—which are not only visually appealing but also often pack a powerful flavor punch—have gained popularity among area chefs, appearing not only as garnish on plates at fine dining restaurants but also as an addition to salads, sandwiches and a wide variety of other dishes. De Stefanis is poised to capitalize on the trend. Current restaurant business includes Locavore and Dream Dance Steak at Potawatomi Hotel & Casino, Bacchus, Lake Park Bistro, Sanford and Amilinda.

The urban farming movement continues to grow. Assistance from community garden grants, chicken and bee ordinances, vacant lot leases, tax breaks for brownfield cleanup and funding for sustainable manufacturing, Milwaukee sets the bar high in terms of post-industrial city evolution.

Chef Driven

The 1990s would be a game changer for Milwaukee, as an increasing number of local chefs and entrepreneurs took an interest in adding their mark to a relatively blank culinary canvas. Pioneers like Marc Bianchini and Brian Zarletti would expand diners' taste for authentic Italian cuisine, while Lake Park Bistro and Coquette Café would introduce the masses to more affordable French bistro fare.

By the early 2000s, chefs who had trained under top chefs like D'Amato and Bartolotta had begun to take an interest in opening their own restaurants. And a new guard was formed. Spots like the Social exposed Milwaukee diners to cuisine that was upscale yet accessible. Roots introduced the city to organic local cuisine. And chefs like Peggy Magister of Crazy Water were empowered to shift diners' focus toward high-quality cuisine served up in more casual environments.

By 2008, Milwaukee's scene had become an anomaly. A downturn in the U.S. economy left many cities mourning the loss of beloved eateries, but Milwaukee's restaurant industry continued to grow, welcoming spots like La Merenda, Hinterland Erie Street Gastropub, Transfer Pizzeria and Umami Moto. And despite all expectations, the growth never slowed.

The evolution of the scene—which now includes a diverse array of both fine dining and casual eateries—is best illustrated through the stories of the culinary visionaries who saw potential on the streets of a once blue-collar town as it struggled to form its identity as a destination for a new age of tourism and industry.

JUSTIN APRAHAMIAN, SANFORD

Chef Justin Aprahamian of Sanford Restaurant.
Photo by Joe Laedtke.

If anyone in Milwaukee understands the concept of sustaining a legacy, it's Justin Aprahamian, chef and owner of Sanford Restaurant.

Aprahamian, who purchased the restaurant from Sanford D'Amato in 2012 with his wife, Sarah, said that it's been an honor to continue the work that D'Amato started. "Sanford, to me, is a hugely important legacy," he said. "And it's bigger than me. It's more than me. It's been twenty-five years, and so many people have come in and out of this building and have helped shape it and push it into what it has become."

Aprahamian got his first taste of the culinary industry at age twelve, when he began helping out with his uncle's catering business. When he entered high school, Aprahamian took a job at Steven Wade's Café in New Berlin, where he started off as a dishwasher and worked his way up to garde manger while earning his culinary degree at Waukesha County Technical College.

"It was always a goal of mine to work at Sanford; the restaurant always represented the next level to me," he said. "Each element of each dish was thoughtfully composed. Everything on the plate had a purpose. But at the same time, I was intimidated by it. So, I really thought of it more as a far-reaching goal. It wasn't until some friends of mine encouraged me to pursue work there that I got up the gumption to apply. I literally got my résumé, put a suit on and knocked on the back door."

Although they weren't advertising for kitchen staff at the time, D'Amato hired Aprahamian. And by the time he turned twenty-one, he found himself working as sous chef of the restaurant he'd dreamed of being a part of for so long. "Sandy was really a great mentor," he said. "And I learned so much from him—so much about composure in the kitchen and focus. There's always a word that comes up among people who have worked here. It's *perspective*. He gave us an amazing amount of it—from his experiences in other restaurants. And it wasn't just about the food. It was about how you treated people."

Aprahamian, who took home the 2014 James Beard Award for Best Chef: Midwest, credited D'Amato with assisting him in exploring the boundaries of what cuisine could be. "Nothing was off limits," he explained. "Anything we wanted to work with, try to make, try to do…it was all fair game. Working with Sandy was about pushing ourselves and pushing the restaurant forward. And that's still how we operate here. We're always trying to dig deeper into our taste memories, to bring things to the surface and create genuinely soulful food."

Two years after taking over full operation of the restaurant, Aprahamian still serves many of the classic dishes for which Sanford became known, including D'Amato's pear and Roquefort tart, his provincial fish soup and grilled fish served with crab hash and pancetta red onion vinaigrette. He's also maintained longtime relationships with vendors at the West Allis Farmers' Market, including Bower's Produce, Westin Orchards and Cindy's Greenhouse in East Troy, which still supplies the baby dumpling squash for Sanford's autumnal squash soup.

But Aprahamian has also begun to put his own stamp on the restaurant's offerings. "It took me a long time to try to work through dishes I thought I wanted to add. But I have been putting more Armenian dishes on the menu—things that are close to home for me and which have influenced my maturation as a cook."

At times, Aprahamian's dishes have forayed into the whimsical. Simple fare like miniature corn dogs and tacos have both been served at the restaurant, as well as at James Beard House events. But they've always been executed with the same care and deliberate discipline as other, more classic fare. "We put the same thought and balance into an *amuse bouche* or a salad as we do with an entrée," he said. "It's about making sure that the dishes make sense and that they're done really well—that they're intentional."

Aprahamian, an avid beer lover—and co-owner of Like Minds Brewing Company—has also made it a point to add to the beer offerings at the restaurant. Once a half-page menu, the Sanford beer list has grown to two full pages, from mainstream brews to specialty cellared options.

"We've always had a nice collection of Belgian brews," he said, "but now we have a larger selection of cellared beers as well as draft beer. The Flying Dog

Gonzo Porter was the first beer I cellared. It was at that point that I started to understand the significance of what beer could be—and that it draws a different audience. To have a larger beer list, and a range of diverse selections, it's providing an experience that you can't just go anywhere and get."

The concept of always giving diners a new experience is embedded in the longtime philosophy at Sanford. "Early on, Sandy was known for very creative combinations and pushing," said Aprahamian. "He was very forward-thinking for the time, so the audience here has expected it. And I've been fortunate to have been immersed in that—to have grown up with it, really."

Along the way, Aprahamian said that he's seen diners grow increasingly receptive to dishes that challenge boundaries. "In Milwaukee, there's definitely been a jump in people's willingness to try new things and push their palates. Through the time I've been here, there are more people throwing caution to the wind and ordering tasting menus. We sell more of those today than we ever have before. And that says a lot about people's willingness to trust the kitchen."

Of course, trusting the kitchen isn't a difficult task, especially when Aprahamian is at the helm.

ADAM SIEGEL, BARTOLOTTA RESTAURANTS

Adam Siegel, corporate chef and managing partner for the Bartolotta Restaurants, grew up in the restaurant industry. Originally intent on going to school for painting and photography, he succumbed to the encouragement of family and opted, instead, to pursue a culinary degree.

After attending Kendall College in Evanston, Illinois, he completed an externship with Paul Bartolotta at Spiaggia in Chicago, a three-month gig that turned into a three-year job. When he left Spiaggia, Siegel spent another three years working with James Beard Award–winning chef Julian Serrano at Masa in San Francisco. At Bartolotta's behest, Siegel took a year to study in Italy before moving to Washington, D.C., where he assisted Todd English in opening a restaurant there. But his Bartolotta ties soon drew him back to Milwaukee.

In 2000, Siegel started his work at Lake Park Bistro as executive sous chef under Chef Mark Weber. He was soon promoted to chef de cuisine, and by 2003, he had been promoted to executive chef. "I put my heart and soul into this place as much as if it were my own," said Siegel of his work with Bartolotta's and at the Bistro in particular. "This is my culinary home. And this food—this simple, rich fare—is very much what I love to cook."

Lake Park Bistro serves French country food—pâtés, sauces and seasonal beef, lamb, veal and poultry dishes. But it's food that improves with practice, and that's Siegel's wheelhouse.

Siegel, who was nominated for the James Beard Best Chef: Midwest award in 2007, and subsequently received the award in 2008, said that his cooking philosophy lies in the perfection of technique. "I love the process. I like to simmer my reductions, while other people will turn up the heat to make them go faster. And the goal is perfecting the dish. Chefs often feel the need

Chef Adam Siegel of Bartolotta Restaurant Group. *Photo by Joe Laedtke.*

to put their stamp on things, but I don't need to change it to be proud. It's delicious the way that it is; it's what it's supposed to be."

Siegel, who has lived and worked in Milwaukee for more than fourteen years, said that he's been a proud contributor to the city's culinary landscape. "The food scene was minute when I arrived," he noted. "Bartolotta's was only three restaurants at that time, and when Paul asked me to come here, I thought I'd be here a year or two at most. It was Milwaukee, and I thought I'd blow in and blow out."

But Siegel's affection for the city grew. "I really learned to love Milwaukee and Wisconsin in general," he said. "There's so much that goes on—the dairy industry, the agriculture, all the different restaurants now, the people and the unique things that are here. It's a fun place and a good place to live."

One of the most rewarding aspects has been his ability to connect with producers. "We have some of the best cheeses in the world, made not more than an hour and a half from here," he said. "It's produced by small farms who are raising their own cows, grasses, and maybe making one or two cheeses. And I can drive there and visit the farmers. I don't think you can do that in New York. It's not that we have more time on our hands, but I'm not fighting traffic to get there."

Siegel described the food scene as "artsy but industrial." "We're really coming around," he said. "I love the fact that we're still kind of pushing back on the national chains. It's a great place to be."

And Siegel said that he's settled in for the long haul. "Lake Park Bistro is twenty years old in September," he noted with a smile. "And it's still going super strong. And I want it to have twenty more years. And why not be a part of that?"

THOMAS HAUCK, C. 1880

It says something about the health of a city's culinary industry when a chef who's been gone for more than twenty years decides to return and put down roots. Such is the case with Thomas Hauck, chef and owner of c. 1880.

A native of the area, Hauck grew up in Port Washington. After graduating from the Culinary Institute of America in Hyde Park, New York, where he completed an externship with Fabio Trabocchi at the Ritz Carleton, Hauck honed his skills in France, training at the Michelin-rated L'Essentiel in Chambéry and then in Perpignan. Upon returning to the States, Hauck worked with Michel Richard at his flagship restaurant, Citronelle, in Washington, D.C.

When he decided to make the leap to open his own restaurant, Hauck took a chance on Milwaukee. "I think everyone wants to go home at some point," he said. "You want to do right by the people you know. And Milwaukee was really moving forward. The quality of life was good. And we saw glimmers of hope in the dining scene—Crazy Water, Hinterland, Lake Park Bistro, Sanford. At the time, Bacchus had just opened. I looked at them and thought, 'If they can make it, we can, too.'"

Hauck took a job at the Pfister Hotel while he learned more about the city, made friends and scouted for locations. When he found a building in Walker's Point that dated back to the 1880s, Hauck was sold. "It was a great time," said Hauck. "Milwaukee was neck and neck with Chicago in the

Chef Thomas Hauck. *Photo by Kevin J. Miyazaki.*

1880s. City hall was the tallest building in the world. We had this epicenter for commerce and agriculture right here, and that inspired me."

Three years later, guests who step into c. 1880 (at 1100 South First Street) are greeted by a cozy, rustic atmosphere filled with reproduction prints of patents and formulas for Tesla's A/C power conversion, pictures depicting Milwaukee farms at the turn of the century and photographs of the city's once thriving shipping and fishing dock at Jones Island. The mood is casual, and the atmosphere is augmented by personal touches, like a tableside visit from Hauck's mother. Much like Charlie Trotter's mother, Dona-Lee, who was known for her stints at the hostess stand, Mary Sue Hauck (Mrs. Hauck to the staff) hosts regularly at c. 1880 on Friday evenings, chatting with guests and making everyone feel like just another member of the family.

The award-winning wine list features an expertly curated selection of both domestic and European wines, including nearly two pages of selections made by esteemed winemakers who hail from Wisconsin. Meanwhile, Hauck's artful and refined menu reflects a respect for seasonal Wisconsin cuisine while pushing the limits of classical technique and presentation.

"It's about showcasing ingredients and reinterpreting them," Hauck said. "When I present you with a dish—no matter how familiar—I want it to be different from what you picture in your mind, but I want it to taste spot-on."

Dishes like Hauck's duck a l'orange showcases duck prepared two ways— confit and cooked *sous vide*—alongside parsnips and turnips that have been diced, shaved and pureed. Monkfish is served atop a sauce made from black olives, fennel and onions and served with orange-braised endive, caramelized fennel, tender scallions and a garnish of chopped olives. And perfectly seared scallops come with white chocolate and sunchoke puree and sliced almonds.

Seasonal foods become edible art as Hauck combines inventive presentation with intermittent flourishes of molecular gastronomy, remaking the familiar into the extraordinary. It's an experience that might seem intimidating if it weren't for the down-to-earth approach Hauck brings to the table. "We're not saving lives—we're cooking dinner."

JUSTIN CARLISLE, ARDENT

If Milwaukee cuisine isn't fully expressed by cheese, sausages and beer, then what is it? One of the answers can be found at Chef Justin Carlisle's restaurant, Ardent.

A born and raised Wisconsinite, Carlisle grew up on a small beef farm in rural Sparta. It was there where he developed a passion and appreciation for the best that the Dairy State had to offer, and it was the land that inspired him to pursue a career in the culinary arts.

Carlisle got off to a running start with experience working at the Greenbrier Resort and Tru Restaurant in Chicago before taking the executive chef positions with Madison restaurants, including Harvest, Muramoto and 43 North. There his work earned him a semifinals nomination for James Beard's Best Chef: Midwest. The following year, Carlisle moved to Chicago to take a post at the Bristol, but before he could get his bearings, SURG snapped him up and brought him to Milwaukee to head up the kitchen at Umami Moto.

Carlisle admitted that he had some reservations about moving to Milwaukee, a city that, in his estimation, didn't have a very good track record for dining. "In the end, I decided there was a lot of untapped opportunity in Milwaukee," he said, "so I gave it a chance. And after living and working here, I really fell in love with the city and the change it was undergoing."

In 2013, Carlisle left Umami Moto to break out on his own. His plan was to open a dual-concept restaurant in the Third Ward that offered diners the choice between casual and fine dining. But when an investor pulled out of the project just before the lease was signed, Carlisle decided to make a go of it himself.

What resulted is Ardent, an intimate chef-driven restaurant where Carlisle makes the most of a minimal kitchen to put out food with maximum impact. "Ardent has been more of what I wanted the whole time," said Carlisle of the nine-hundred-square-foot garden-level restaurant that opened in October 2013. "Working into that was the concept of less is more. We don't have hoods.

Chef Justin Carlisle of Ardent. *Photo by Joe Laedtke.*

We don't have gas. We can do a lot more here in the city and state if we just concentrate on what we really need and not just what we want."

Carlisle's concept, which he executes with the help of chef colleagues Aaron Patin and Matt Haase, capitalizes on his experiences growing up on the beef farm, surrounded by the bounty of Wisconsin agriculture. "We lived the culture of growing our own and preserving and eating what we produced," he said. "And little did I know when I was ten years old that this was going to be the biggest trend in the world."

It's tradition and memory that drive the ingenuity on Ardent's menu, through which Carlisle reinterprets familiar Wisconsin ingredients and dishes in modern, often unexpected ways. One dish on the menu, simply named "Milk," features a wooden plank topped with a thick slice of butter, a wedge of cheese and a *pan au lait*—all three components made from the milk Carlisle picked up earlier in the week from Edelweiss Creamery in Green County. It's a symbol of the way Carlisle thinks about food and cooking.

"For me, it's about the thought process that goes into the food," said Carlisle. "And it all goes back to basics. How can we understand things now if we don't understand what came before us?"

Carlisle gets beef from his father's farm, where he takes an active role in how the animals are raised and how they live. Vegetables are sourced with similar care from nearby farms and foragers, most of whom approach their work with a similar intensity to that of Carlisle. "It's about attention to detail," said Carlisle. "We're able to pick at the right time, pickle at the right time, store at the right time. And serve at the right time."

That dedication earned Carlisle a semifinalist nomination for the 2015 James Beard Best Chef: Midwest award, as well as a mention among "30 Chefs to Watch" by *Plate* magazine. Similarly, Ardent received acclaim as a semifinalist for Best New Restaurant in the Country by the James Beard Foundation in 2014 and has been listed among the "Top 15 New Restaurants in the Midwest" by *Condé Nast Traveler*.

"People said you couldn't put a restaurant like Ardent in Milwaukee— that it wouldn't work," Carlisle remarked. "But we did. In the end, it's just further proof of how great this city is and how it's being settled like the final frontier in the culinary world."

Beginning in 2014, Carlisle also launched a popular after-hours business at Ardent. Red Light Ramen serves up house-made ramen with accompaniments like soy-marinated soft-boiled eggs, nori, bamboo shoots and pickled wasabi greens on Friday and Saturday evenings starting at 11:30 p.m. The underground concept, which caters to late-night foodies and industry folks, has earned its own set of accolades, including a 2015 appearance on the Travel Channel's *Man Finds Food* with Adam Richman.

MIKE ENGEL, PASTICHE

Sometimes a dream comes true when a chef returns to the basics. And such was the case for Mike Engel, chef-owner of Pastiche Bistro and Wine Bar, whose wish to own his own restaurant was nearly thirty years in the making.

Engel started out as so many chefs do: washing dishes in a busy restaurant kitchen. From there, he held jobs at the Bavarian Inn and the Milwaukee Country Club, where he took on a live-in apprenticeship while working his way through culinary school at Milwaukee Area Technical College. "The chefs were German by nationality, but the food was classic Escoffier French,"

Mike Engel of Pastiche. *Photo by Joe Laedtke.*

remembered Engel. "So there was a lot of technique. I learned so much, and it instilled an overarching love for French food and wine."

From there, he earned his stripes at the Bluemound Country Club and then Tripoli Country Club, where he worked his way up from sous to executive chef before opening the Wooden Eagle Bar and Grill for Bob Lang in Delafield and the Hotel Metro for legendary culinarian and designer Madame Kuony.

"Madame Kuony was an impresario," recalled Engel. "She used to bring me various things to cook at the Wooden Eagle. She'd bring her driver over with bags, and I'd prepare food for her parties. My two-year run at the Metro was one of the high points of my career. I loved coming to work. It was challenging. And I was working with some of the best people I could imagine at the time. We were making good food and getting recognition for it."

In 2000, the hotel changed direction, and Engel lost his position as chef. Disheartened, he made a fresh start by going to work for Joe Bartolotta and assisting him in launching their catering division. When Bob Lang decided to relaunch the Wooden Eagle in 2003, Engel begrudgingly submitted. "Every ounce of intelligence I had said it was a dumb idea. But my heart overruled my head. My ex-wife and sons were living within three blocks of the restaurant, so I thought I'd see my kids more. But ultimately, it fell apart."

Engel moved on to take a corporate chef position with Quad Graphics, where he supervised food service for five of their plants, as well as prepared meals in the Quadraccis' home, trains and aircraft. He moved on to work with the owners of Legend of Brandybrook, a new private golf course in Wales, assisting them with kitchen design, developing infrastructure and eventually overseeing the food and beverage operations at all three of their properties. "Ultimately, I really missed cooking," said Engel. "I was tired of working for other people and making money for them. I called my kids and asked if they were interested in working in a restaurant if I opened one. And they were."

So, Engel created a business plan. In 2009, money was hard to find. But Engel lucked out when a friend from the banking industry offered to give him a loan. "I've never had a feeling like it in my life," Engel recalled. "Freedom. Optimism. I was overwhelmed with feeling, knowing that I was going to get to do something I loved."

What he loved was simple, rustic French fare. Cassoulet. Coq au vin. Escargot. Ratatouille. Frogs' legs. And, in 2010, Pastiche in Bay View became the canvas for Engel's passion. The restaurant, which opened in April, met with immediate popularity, thanks to both Engel's talent and favorable reviews from the media. And within months, the forty-eight-seat restaurant was a neighborhood institution.

Even five years later, Engel's seasonal menu of traditional French bistro dishes, along with weekly specials, continues to make Pastiche a bustling destination, where diners without reservations are lucky if they can find an open seat at the bar on weekends. "We're not cutting edge. We're not trendy," said Engel. "We make solid, simple French food in the best way we can with the best ingredients we can find."

For some, it's a simple dream. But for Engel, it's everything. "This is where I want to be," he said. "And I want to keep on doing what I'm doing until I die—happily—at the stove."

BRIAN ZARLETTI, ZARLETTI

Brian Zarletti didn't grow up far from Milwaukee. In fact, he got his start about thirty miles south in Kenosha. "I started waiting tables in a good Italian restaurant, Villa D' Carlo on the harbor," said Zarletti. "I was young and it was fun. And it was there that I caught the bug."

Zarletti went on to work at Racine's Main Street Bistro, owned by the Leipolds, who were partners with the Levys in Spiaggia in Chicago. "Back in the day, Spiaggia was *it*," he said. "So in the early 1990s, that was a real wakeup for me. We were using things that I'd never had before— veal sweetbreads, soft-shelled crab. At the time, there was no Food Network, so we hadn't seen things like this in the Midwest. It was a great education and got me very, very interested in Italian food at a high level."

A few years later, Zarletti moved to South Milwaukee, where he opened a flower shop with his former wife. Eventually, he added a coffee shop. And then he got the urge to do more. So, he

Brian Zarletti of Zarletti's, Zarletti Mequon, Rustico and Stubby's Gastropub & Beer Bar. *Photo by Joe Laedtke.*

opened a small restaurant called Café Zarletti. "I started traveling to Italy and augmenting my palate with real, authentic Italian cooking," he said. "The more I learned, the more I respected my grandmother—who was first-generation American—and her sense of the cuisine. Once I started traveling, I realized how a lot of the food that was served in Italian restaurants in the Midwest was really being created from an Italian-American sensibility."

In his quest to reproduce a more authentic cuisine, he experienced hits and misses. He also found that the location of the café simply didn't have enough regular customers to be sustainable. So, Zarletti began looking for a new location. When he happened upon the building on Milwaukee Street, which held Crescent City Beignets, he knew that it would be a good move. "There wasn't much there at the time," he recalled. "There was a coffee shop, Hotel Metro, Eve, Tangerine. There was a cheese shop in the space that would eventually house Cubanitas. And Umami Moto was under construction."

The opening menu at Zarletti in 2004 showcased rustic Northern Italian fare like osso buco and pan-seared salmon. And it evolved from there, expanding as Zarletti learned more about the cuisine. "Despite the evolution of the restaurant, we've always set out to be value-driven," he said. "And our focus has always been on quality food that doesn't necessarily aim to push boundaries. Instead, we've stayed true to the notion of dishes that have been created in the kitchens of Italian nonnas for hundreds of years."

Although he started out in the kitchen, Zarletti eventually transitioned himself into more of a front-of-the-house role. "The kitchen is the heart of a restaurant," he said. "And I've always been all about the food, but I soon realized how the front of the house is vital to the operation. I also learned that there were people who could much more effectively execute the dishes I'd envisioned."

And Zarletti has kept that notion in mind, even as he's expanded his restaurant ownership to include Rustico (2007), Stubby's Gastropub & Beer Bar with Brad Todd (2010) and Zarletti Mequon (2014). "When we first opened, we had to tell people what osso buco was," Zarletti recalled. "We had to explain ingredients like prosciutto, pancetta. Those things just weren't common. These days, you can get fresh mozzarella in four different shapes at the grocery store. So, little by little, the goal has become broadening people's view of what Italian food really is, how diverse it is."

COLE ERSEL, WOLF PEACH

When you look at the range of executive-level chefs in Milwaukee, Cole Ersel is among the youngest. He took over the role as executive chef at just twenty-five and has proven himself a worthy contributor to the city's culinary talent. Wolf Peach maintains the farm-to-table philosophy of its predecessor, Roots, serving up an evolving selection of rustic European-inspired fare, along with pizzas and entrées prepared in the restaurant's wood-fired oven.

The restaurant, perched above the city on Brewer's Hill, sports a beautiful view of downtown Milwaukee, luring customers with its pristine garden and open-air patio. "We offer Milwaukee diners a really diverse experience," said Ersel. "You can come in and get bone marrow. Or vegan fare. Or gluten-free food. You can get a bowl of Brussels sprouts with grapes and shallots. Or have a pizza. It's really our goal not to leave anyone out."

Chef Cole Ersel of Wolf Peach. *Photo by Joe Laedtke.*

Ersel, who began his career working in restaurants in Chicago and then Denver, returned to Milwaukee in 2010, as the city's dining landscape was really beginning to bloom. "I thought that Denver's food scene was up and coming," said Ersel. "But when I came back here, I discovered that Milwaukee was actually one step ahead. Agriculture-wise, the sheer amount of food being produced in the area really gave Wisconsin a leg up."

Ersel landed a position in the kitchen at SURG's Carnevor, working with experienced chefs Jarvis Williams and Dane Baldwin. In the morning, before his restaurant shifts began, he'd assist Distil chef Matt Haase (now employed at Ardent) with breaking down animals for the restaurant. As he developed more of a taste for working with meat, he moved on to Hinterland, where he worked with chef and charcuterie expert Paul Funk before accepting a position working with Executive Chef Daniel Jacobs at Roots.

"At that point, I was starting to feel pretty confident with the butchery," he said. "So I suggested we start a butchery program. And that was very much a learning curve for me. I was twenty-two years old and was bringing in $600 hogs and breaking them down and really honing my skills in charcuterie."

When Roots closed five or six months down the road, reopening a few months later as Wolf Peach, Ersel continued on in his role for the first year. Then he decided he needed a break. He accepted a position in the

Brown butter sunchoke ravioli with spinach puree, sunchoke chips and parsley garlic tuile. Dish by Cole Ersel of Wolf Peach. *Photo by Joe Laedtke.*

kitchen at Morel, a restaurant scheduled to open in Walker's Point months down the road. While he was waiting for the restaurant to be remodeled, he headed south.

After returning to Milwaukee from a walkabout on the Appalachian Trail, he butted up against the opportunity of a lifetime. Jacobs was leaving Wolf Peach to work at Odd Duck. And owner Gina Gruenewald was looking for a new executive to replace him. Ersel decided to apply. "I don't think it would have worked if I hadn't already been so involved at Roots and Wolf Peach," he remarked. "I knew the staff. I knew the food. I had my hands in everything enough that it gave me a shot at it."

Ersel credited the chef community in Milwaukee with creating a supportive atmosphere where he could thrive. "I had all these friends who I could ask for help," he said. "And I walked into Wolf Peach with a really strong crew. Kyle Toner, Daniel Pope, Andrew Squire—they've all been executive chefs and their résumés are stronger than mine—so I lean on those guys. And they lift me up."

Jan Kelly, Meritage

Chef Jan Kelly remembered a time when the nine-course dinners at her parents' fine dining restaurant, the Hobbit in Orange, California, cost $14.95 per person. These days, at the restaurant her brother now manages, a seven-course version costs more than five times that. "I grew up around the food," said Kelly. "Both of my parents were self-taught chefs, and they taught me to embrace all types of food—French, Mexican, Japanese. I loved food, but I didn't know I liked cooking."

But when Kelly started working at the Hobbit, managing books and doing kitchen prep, she found it satisfying. So she began exploring other kitchens, including one belonging to a classically trained French chef in Orange County. "It was the 1970s, and there were no women chefs," she said. "Women worked the salad station and maybe made desserts. But the chef worked with me, taught me. It was such a great experience. That was the catalyst for me. If that hadn't happened, I probably wouldn't have gone on."

Kelly decided against culinary school, opting instead for hands-on practical work in a variety of California kitchens, ultimately taking on the role of chef at the Hobbit. When she married Gary, a University of Wisconsin–Milwaukee alum and former speed skater who had trained at the

Jan Kelly of Meritage. *Photo by Joe Laedtke.*

Olympic ice rink in Milwaukee, the couple traveled to Milwaukee to visit some old friends and Kelly fell in love.

"The people were so nice, and the food was really interesting," she said. "I'd come here, and we'd go to these little funky places—Mader's and Karl Ratzsch's—and eat delicious German food and bratwurst. And I remember going to Sanford and thinking, 'Wow!' It was like dining out in California."

In 1995, Kelly and her husband moved to Milwaukee. She worked at the Delafield House, North Shore Bistro and then the Knick before moving on to Barossa, a restaurant in Walker's Point owned by Julia Deloggia and Deanne Wecker that specialized in organic, local food. "California has a large amount of farming, so the concept of sourcing always seemed natural to me. We used to always get stuff. It was easy, it was there…it was grown there. But I never thought about where it came from. I just ordered it."

In Milwaukee, Kelly got to know the farmers. "For me, the most important thing became, 'Where does it come from? And how locally can we get it?'" she said. "I streamlined the Barossa menu, and we started working with more local purveyors. And I loved it. I loved talking to them and getting to know them, learning from them."

Shortly before Barossa closed, Kelly took a leap of faith and opened her own place. "Everything we looked at in Bay View, which was the hot spot at the time, was a build-out," she recalled. "And I really wanted something more turnkey."

When the owners of Indigo, a restaurant in her Washington Heights neighborhood, decided to sell, Kelly jumped on it. Her goal was to offer patrons a fine dining experience, complete with quality service; beautiful, well-composed food; and wine for a reasonable price. "Dining isn't going out to eat anymore. It's entertainment," she said. "We're meeting friends, trying new foods, experiencing something. So I think it's important that the entire thing—from beginning to end—is packaged well."

Customers who knew Kelly from her work at Barossa flocked to the new restaurant, which opened in August 2007 with menu items like bison meatloaf and halibut served over Moroccan lentils with saffron. Kelly maintained her relationships with the purveyors and farms she'd worked with at Barossa—places like Pin-Oak Ridge Farms, Growing Power and Yuppie Hill Poultry. "Ten years ago, you saw a lot less farm-to-table dining. It was difficult for farmers to produce enough to sustain restaurants. But I was one of a group of chefs who worked with them and gave them a market for what they had, and together we built a network of suppliers."

Along the way, Kelly encouraged other restaurant owners to buy produce from vendors like Growing Power—even if it was just one item—to assist them in building their business. She also connected with Dave Swanson and became one of the founding members of his RSA program. "Today it's just an expectation that restaurants will make local fare with local food," she said. "But it took time to grow into that and for the networks to form to really make it possible."

As the years passed, Kelly's menus began to reflect more internationally inspired fare, and Meritage developed a reputation for its creative use of local products. On any given evening, diners might see lamb moussaka on the menu alongside an autumn bouillabaisse or sweet potato gnocchi, each made with a selection of locally procured ingredients. By 2012, Kelly had been nominated as a semifinalist for the James Beard Best Chef: Midwest.

Kelly said that one of the most enjoyable aspects of being part of the dining scene in Milwaukee is the chef community that has formed over the years. "I've always felt really welcome, and I really enjoy working with other chefs. Having a support group is always good, and that's really what we've formed. In 2014, when it was so cold and everyone was hurting because no one was going out, we all went out. We ate at one another's restaurants. We supported one another. And that's what it's about."

Peggy Magister, Crazy Water and AP Bar and Kitchen

Sitting in the Crazy Water dining room watching Chef Peggy Magister at work on a busy evening is a sight to behold. It's almost a blur as staff whisk ingredients from prep to pan and onto plate. But the motions are fluid, and the timing is as perfect as it needs to be when they're serving up artful dishes from the helm of a ten- by ten-foot open kitchen.

Crazy Water has been a fixture at 839 South Second Street in Walker's Point since 2002, when Magister and Tony Betzhold snatched up the former home of a German bar, Zur Krone, and transformed it into a Milwaukee institution. "At the time, I wanted to bring something to the city," said Magister. "I wanted to contribute. Not many people were doing California-style cuisine. And the restaurant was small enough that I didn't need many people to fill it, so I held my breath and hoped people would embrace it."

Chef Peggy Magister of Crazy Water. *Photo by Joe Laedtke.*

And embrace it they did. The restaurant's reputation for impeccable, inventive comfort food attracted diners from across the city in the days before the Walker's Point neighborhood became known as a dining destination. More than a decade later, the menu at Crazy Water still attracts a crowd. Starters like yuzu-marinated pork belly, chorizo-stuffed dates and escargot in tomato *concassé* sit alongside signature main dishes like grilled flat-iron steak and "crazy shrimp," a dish featuring Asian barbecue-sauced shrimp served with chorizo and tomatoes over rice with jalapeño corn bread muffins.

Magister, who started her career as a nurse, switched gears when she was thirty and decided to go to cooking school. "I'd always wanted to cook, but that hadn't been an option for me starting out," she recalled. "But at that point in my life I was single, with no ties to anything aside from my family, so I went for it."

Magister attended the California Culinary Academy in San Francisco. While she went to school, she got a job working with Wolfgang Puck at his restaurant Postrio. "When I finished school, I realized that to really get ahead, I'd have to come home," Magister said. "It was too expensive to make it in California."

Magister returned to Milwaukee, where she worked at Steven Wade's Café as well as Chip & Pye's in Mequon. That's where she met Betzhold. He and Magister started a catering company together, along with the Fork Café, a boulangerie in Cedarburg. But when the restaurant wasn't doing as well as Magister had hoped, she decided to move to Milwaukee. "I worked at the Knick—it was a new thing at the time—and at North Shore Bistro," she said. "I think part of why I opened my new place was that, ultimately, I didn't have the confidence to work somewhere else. I just wouldn't have applied with Bartolotta's or at Sanford."

As she looked for locations to start a restaurant, she said that she wasn't particular about location, although she was inspired by restaurants like the Social, which had popped up in Walker's Point, a neighborhood that hadn't yet earned a reputation for being a dining destination. "I really just wanted someplace I could cook and make a living doing it," she said. "So when we found the spot in Walker's Point, I took it. And I learned how to make it work."

Betzhold handled the business end of things, and Magister did the cooking. And business took off. "I really couldn't have done it without Tony," she said. "He knew the business much better than I did. And we were best friends."

By 2012, Beard Award nominee Magister found herself growing restless. "I was kind of bored," she said. "And I got it in my head that I wanted to do tapas." Meanwhile, a property near Crazy Water had become available, and her nephew, Justin Anthony, who had been working in the service industry in Boulder, Colorado, expressed an interest in moving back home. "He had a lot of experience, and as I'd talk with him, I realized he really knew what he was talking about. So we decided to do it together."

AP Bar and Kitchen opened in 2013. It was the small-plates restaurant that Magister had envisioned, with menu items like fried catfish with malt vinegar, sweetbreads, baby octopus panzanella salad and fried chicken with soy ginger vinaigrette and kimchee. There was an oyster bar, craft cocktails and an expertly curated wine list focused on European-style wines.

But ultimately, Magister said, it wasn't her dream. So, after two years, she turned the reins over to Anthony and decided to refocus her efforts on Crazy Water. "This is another generation, another food craze, and this new era belongs to them," she said. "It's their turn to try their hand at changing the food scene."

Magister feels that it's good to be back in the kitchen. But, she said, as she and her clientele get older, she struggles with how to remain relevant. "I'm here every day. I'm hands-on and I don't have any managers. But I'm at a challenging place right now. There's only so much dining public, and yet I'm looking around, and all the restaurants are so flippin' good. All I can do is to keep working hard. Concentrate. Be here. And do the best I can."

DAN VAN RITE, HINTERLAND ERIE STREET GASTROPUB

There may not be a more low-key chef in the city of Milwaukee than Dan Van Rite. But don't let his quiet, unassuming nature fool you. He's a beast in the kitchen. As executive chef for Hinterland Erie Street Gastropub, Van Rite is the man behind an ever-changing menu of internationally inspired wild game, fresh fish and seafood dishes. The emphasis is on fresh and seasonal, with ingredients sourced from the area's best growers, grazers and foragers.

A 2012 copy of the menu reads, "This all started long before you walked in. Before your arrival here, rich soil was turned. Produce was nurtured, grown and harvested. Local farmers tended to their pastoral landscapes and

Chef Dan Van Rite of Hinterland Erie Street Gastropub. *Photo by Joe Laedtke.*

livestock. Fish plucked from the briny depths arrived this very morning. All in preparation for you to walk through our doors."

Most people don't know that Van Rite started out aspiring to be an architect. In fact, it's what he started studying when he moved to Milwaukee from Green Bay in 1989. But ultimately, he chose another path. He quit school and took a job working at Beans & Barley on Milwaukee's East Side. "That was my first experience on the line," Van Rite recalled. "I was at the point in my life where I didn't know where I wanted to live, but I did know I didn't want to sit in an architect's chair all day long. I wanted to be active. Cooking, on the other hand, was something I enjoyed. It made me happy. It also gave me the freedom to go wherever I wanted."

Van Rite moved to Portland, Oregon, where he attended the Western Culinary Institute and absorbed as much information as he could. After interning at the Caribou Club in Aspen, Colorado, he returned to Portland for nearly three years before taking a job back in Colorado at the Marvine Ranch in Meeker. It was seasonal work, so Van Rite found himself using his extra time to travel. He worked in Florida and Minneapolis and made plans to move to Telluride. "Ultimately, I couldn't find anywhere that would let me keep my dog," he said. So he moved back home to Green Bay in 2000.

At the time, Bill Tressler was looking for a chef to head up the kitchen at his new Hinterland Brewery restaurant in Green Bay. He offered the job to Van Rite, who stayed at the restaurant for five years before taking a position as a personal chef for a family in New York.

In 2008, Tressler lured Van Rite back to Wisconsin by asking him to return as executive chef for his new Milwaukee restaurant, Hinterland Erie Street Gastropub. "The restaurant had been open for about four months when I started," says Van Rite. "The recession hit later that year, and we took a pretty big hit. But after that, the buzz got going."

By 2012, Van Rite was a three-time James Beard semifinalist for Best Chef: Midwest. And the accolades for his rustic American fare earned him a trusted reputation. "People ask me, 'How did the menu come about?'" Van Rite said. "It was really inspired by my traveling. In Colorado, game was really big. Friends and family were hunters. My love for seafood came from experiences on the East and West Coasts. That whole range of coastal experiences came together."

Van Rite flies in fresh seafood from Honolulu, Seattle and Portland, Maine. He sources game from small farms and ranches. And when it comes to produce, Van Rite said that he tries to support as many farms and foragers as he can. "Peter Sandroni [at La Merenda] turned me on to Turtle Creek

Farm and Pinehold Gardens," he said. "I use Jeff Leen for eggs. Receiving product is my favorite thing. It gets me the most excited. I mean, you order stuff from a farm, and it comes in. You walk in and you see it all, and your brain starts processing all of it…I have this, and this…and I can do this and this. It gives me creativity. I'm more creative when I just look at what I have, instead of just sitting and coming up with a dish."

Van Rite also credited his kitchen staff with keeping things fresh and pushing the restaurant forward. "I have a mix of young and eager and old and mature. There's more talent here now. Young culinary students and people who've moved here. It's good—much better than when I first got here."

Van Rite's menu is in a constant state of evolution, and weekly changes are the rule rather than the exception. It's part of what diners have come to expect from Hinterland. But it's also part of what keeps Van Rite going. "You're never doing the same things over and over again," he said. "It's about keeping the menu new and creative and constantly getting better and better. I never want things to get stagnant and boring."

KAREN BELL, BAVETTE LA BOUCHERIE

If you round the corner at the southern end of Broadway Street in Milwaukee's Third Ward, you'll come upon one of the Cream City's most unique eateries, Bavette La Boucherie. Chef Karen Bell's butcher shop and café maintains a sharp focus on quality, locally sourced and sustainably raised meats.

After earning her culinary degree from Milwaukee Area Technical College, Bell studied at Le Cordon Bleu in Paris and then cut her culinary teeth in Chicago, where she worked as head line cook at Vong Restaurant and later as pastry cook at Charlie Trotter's. After working for three years at San Francisco's Farallon, she ventured to Madrid, where she eventually opened the California-inspired restaurant Memento. The thirty-seat restaurant, which earned Bell a reputation as "Spain's Alice Waters," built a successful following thanks to skillfully prepared food and well-curated wine, along with innovative concepts like "jazz brunch" on Sundays and a high-end *menú del día* (*prix fixe*) lunch. But after a few years, the work grew exhausting. "When I first left Spain, I thought I would never, ever start my own restaurant again," she said. "I had done everything myself, and I was burnt out."

So, Bell moved back to her hometown and entered into a consulting agreement with Café at the Plaza, where she eventually became executive chef. "Meanwhile, I was discovering Milwaukee and finding out that it had become a really cool place. I also realized that I had become the type of person who needed to own what I was doing."

Bell toyed with the idea of opening a Spanish restaurant, but an early summer visit to Publican Quality Meats, a traditional but contemporary butcher shop and restaurant in Chicago, changed her tune. "I was getting really interested in butchery," she said. "And all at once, my concept morphed into this idea of a butcher shop with a café. It was something Milwaukee didn't have—something it needed. And that made me excited."

As part of her research, Bell staged at a few butcher shops in Chicago, including the Butcher and Larder. She spent a great

Karen Bell of Bavette La Boucherie. *Photo by Joe Laedtke.*

deal of time reading and studying and practicing her techniques. She was also lucky enough to make the acquaintance of Bill Kreitmeier, a longtime butcher whose résumé included work at Grasch's, Groppi's and his own shop at the Milwaukee Public Market.

When Bell opened Bavette in 2013, Kreitmeier became one of her most valued employees. "It's great to have Bill here because he has so much knowledge," Bell explained. "We were able to merge our sausage recipes and techniques. He is more old school, and I'm more into fresh garlic and herbs. It's a great match."

Bell said that her inspiration for the boucherie came from an increasing interest in food politics, as well as her desire to assist Milwaukeeans in reconnecting with their food. "I saw lots of people shopping at the farmers' market and being concerned with where their vegetables were coming from.

But there wasn't much talk about sustainably raised meat. I thought it would be a good way to connect people with farmers producing that sort of meat."

Nose-to-tail is Bell's operating philosophy, and it plays directly into the way she handles her business. "We are a restaurant, but we're also a butcher shop," said Bell, "and that brings with it some advantages. It's tough for a restaurant to go through a side of beef, but we don't have that issue because we do both."

Food in the café, the flavors of which often resemble finer dining, includes charcuterie, soups, salads and sandwiches, with each dish taking direction from seasonal produce and the meats available at the shop. "At this point, I know that the brisket doesn't sell, so we have a lot of things on the menu with brisket," said Bell. "Pork belly is another thing. We do braised or roast beef because we have a round to use up."

Bell also works with her suppliers to help them get rid of extra less popular cuts. "I like the challenge of figuring out what to do with different things. I like cooking that way. Same with produce. I like creating a menu on the basis of what we can get during the week."

She credited the growth of the Milwaukee dining scene with making it possible to do what she does. "People are starting to push the envelope," she noted. "At first, there were many items I put on the menu that I didn't necessarily expect to sell. But I've been pleasantly surprised by the increased sophistication diners are bringing to the table. It's a really fun time to be working in Milwaukee."

JOE MUENCH, BLACK SHOE HOSPITALITY

There are few Milwaukeeans who work harder than Joe Muench, chef and co-owner of the Black Shoe Hospitality group. And he's been working long days in the city since he was fifteen years old.

Muench was raised on Seventy-seventh and Wisconsin Avenue, not far from where his three restaurants now stand. While he was in high school, the now-accomplished chef maintained a paper route and a job at a local gas station.

His love for all things culinary stems back to childhood—watching his grandmother cook and bake and catching episodes of *The Frugal Gourmet* on public television. "Jeff Smith captivated me," said Muench. "His approach is so simple, and he gives you a lot of history. I don't know how he'd fit into today's scene—he's not really flashy enough. But I learned a lot from him."

Muench's first job in the service industry was at Marty's Pizza on Greenfield Avenue, where he recalled the challenge of making five-foot-long pizzas. "It was nonstop go," he said with a smile. "I did everything from cooking to delivering. To this day, it's still my favorite job."

After a stint in college, Muench switched gears and decided to go the route of culinary school. He worked at Perkins while he attended Milwaukee Area Technical College and then Houlihan's at Brookfield Square before landing a job as a line cook at Grenadier's. "That was 1990," Muench recalled. "I'd started a family early, and I was eager to get a career going. I worked at Grenadier's on Monday

Chef Joe Muench of Black Shoe Hospitality. *Photo by Joe Laedtke.*

through Thursday nights, Friday during the day and Saturday in the evening. I was at Perkins on the weekends: Saturday very early morning and Sunday day, as well. Between school and work, my only nights off were Friday and Sunday."

He started at Grenadier's preparing vegetables and side dishes but eventually moved up to sous chef, a role that gave him a solid opportunity to learn from one of Milwaukee's best chefs, Knut Apitz, for nearly five years. The experience gave him skills in handling work in a high-volume, fine-dining kitchen, where customer service was key. "Any night of the week at Grenadier's, you'd have fifteen to twenty selections of fish," he recalled. "And at least half of what went out of the kitchen was a special order or request. And that was in addition to what was on the menu."

Years later, his experience creating a wide variety of custom dishes would inspire Muench to offer up myriad daily specials at Maxie's, Blue's Egg and Story Hill BKC, restaurants known for their creativity and diverse offerings.

When he was just twenty-four, Muench was hired to open Eddie Martini's, an upscale chophouse concept where his sense of frugality in the kitchen, having learned to make the best use of every ingredient, gave him a one-up on other applicants. From there, he moved on to work at a country club in Lake Geneva, as well as Sticks 'n' Stones and the Chancery, restaurants owned by Joe DeRosa. It was at the Chancery where he met Dan Sidner, who would eventually become his business partner.

In 2007, Sidner partnered up with Chick Evans to open Maxie's, a southern-themed restaurant where they hired Muench as executive chef. The restaurant, which served up dishes like jambalaya and po-boys, settled into a spot at the corner of Sixty-eighth and Fairview Avenue, the former home of Gerry O'Brien's Meat Market. "It was good timing for the concept," Muench recalled. "Comfort food was coming back in the post-9/11 world, and it was really a good fit for Milwaukee at the time."

The restaurant did well, and two years later, when Sidner decided to sever ties with Evans, he brought Muench on as a partner. The two started brainstorming concepts for a second restaurant, most likely a breakfast spot next door to Maxie's.

Around the same time, it was announced that Peggy and John Byron Burns would be closing their beloved Heinemann's Restaurants, which had been in business since 1923. One of the locations at Seventy-sixth and Bluemound turned out to be perfect for the new project. "Milwaukee really had no good breakfast joints at the time," said Muench. "But Heinemann's had been serving a breakfast and lunch crowd for more than forty years in that location. We were humbled by the legacy but also determined to pay tribute by continuing their work."

In 2010, Sidner and Muench launched Blue's Egg, a breakfast and lunch spot that combined elements of fine dining with food inspired by American immigrant populations. The menu went beyond eggs and bacon, serving up dishes like crab cakes, seafood scramble, Hoppel Poppel and stuffed hash browns. And it became popular for its ever-changing specials and sometimes zany themes. Soon there were lines out the door. And "Blue's" became known as the best spot in Milwaukee to grab breakfast or brunch.

Blue's success made Sidner and Muench a sought-after pair, and soon there were talks with the local aldermen about yet another space that needed some love. This time, it was a uniform shop on West Bluemound Road in Story Hill. "We'll never open a place just to open a place," said Muench. "We want to impact and change neighborhoods, move into an area that's underserved. And that was what we did."

It was risky proposition, but the two hatched a plan to open a combination coffee shop/restaurant/wine and beer shop. Construction began in February 2014. In less than a year, Story Hill BKC (aka Bottle Kitchen Cup) offered Milwaukeeans access to quick-service fare, as well as sit-down dining and a retail space where they can find and take home wine and beer, including growlers of BKC draft options.

A breakfast menu features crepes, frittatas and more inventive dishes like *shakshouka*, while lunch features a small selection of soups, salads and sandwiches. Dinner revolves around the concept of "taste, share and pass"—offering small plates like escargot and cheese plates; larger shareable plates including burrata with jam, pesto and balsamic reduction and pan-seared sturgeon and family-style dishes like country spareribs and cheese and potato agnolotti.

The concept is still evolving, changing hours to match customer habits and customizing fare to appeal to local palates. But in his traditional fashion, Muench is up to the task, and he's already looking forward to figuring out what's next. "We're focused on getting really good at what we're doing," he said. "I've spent a lot of time getting restaurants up and going in the past few years. Now I'm focusing on reeducating myself."

Nell Benton, National Café

Once upon a time, there was a small café on National Avenue. Founded on the notions of community and sustainability, the café served up fresh local breakfast and lunch fare in an atmosphere of congeniality and activism.

On any given morning, passersby would be likely to find a handful of neighborhood folks sipping coffee and discussing the latest in local news and views, area politicians and business owners coming together for a coffee meeting or artists grabbing a bite to eat between projects.

But in 2011, the National Café—which had been founded by owner Michael Diedrick three years before—was in need of a new owner. Committed to finding a buyer who would maintain the original intent of the café, most notably its commitment to both sustainability and the surrounding neighborhood, Diedrick interviewed a wide range of candidates, listening to their visions and allowing them to express their level of commitment to each of eleven conditions for the space, staff and mission.

Nell Benton answered the call. Benton, who grew up in Green Bay, traveled extensively and earned her culinary degree at the Art Institute in Fort

Nell Benton of the National Café. *Photo by Joe Laedtke.*

Lauderdale, Florida. When she moved back to Milwaukee in 2010 to be closer to family, she worked at a number of restaurants, including Saz's and Thirst & Vine in Shorewood, where she wrote a new menu for the restaurant.

Having lived and worked in a variety of culinary meccas—most notably London, the French-influenced British isle of Jersey, Cairo and Indonesia—she brought a global perspective to the restaurant, as well as a load of energy to keep the spirit of the space going. "It was a really cute space," Benton recalled. "I liked the old building, and the staff were really nice. I do remember thinking it was really, really small."

One of the first tasks Benton took up was changing the menu, adding selections that reflected her culinary expertise, as well as options inspired by her international travel. She added more morning fare, including breakfast sliders, a Croque Madame and the "Full English" featuring sunny-side-up eggs, English bangers, tomatoes, mushrooms, potatoes, beans and toast.

Lunch boasts a multitude of sandwiches and salads, including lemon caper tuna salad; the popular turkey, bacon and brie panini; and a crisp baguette with seared pork belly, smeared with Sriracha mayo. There are also traditional options like grilled cheese, egg salad and ham and cheese.

In 2013, Benton took lunch service a step further, adding *Tonkotsu* ramen to the menu. House-made alkaline noodles bathe in a rich stock made from pork feet, chicken bones and smoked pork hocks, a "secret" ingredient that offers up a subtle smoky flavor. The ramen is augmented by pork belly, scallions, nori, a soy-marinated soft-boiled egg and fresh sweet corn. It also comes with an optional "spicy bomb"—a mix of *sambal* and Sriracha that has the capacity to warm up even the chilliest diners.

Benton took the opportunity to establish a robust catering operation, offering not only sandwiches and salads but also more creative options like breakfast stations and a ramen bar. For Benton, community outreach is top of mind, and she serves breakfast at local farmers' markets and is involved in neighborhood improvement efforts. In 2012, she also teamed up with Thi Cao, formerly of Buckley's Restaurant and Bar, to form a chefs' collaborative called Milwaukee Food for Thought, a series of quarterly dinners that raise funds for charitable organizations. Meals are held somewhere in Milwaukee and feature themed courses, each created by a different chef.

The first Food for Thought Dinner—an offal-themed dinner affectionately referred to as "Nasty Bits"—paid homage to longtime Grenadier's chef Knut Apitz, raising money for the Wisconsin Parkinson's Association. It featured creative dishes like a triad of veal brains, lamb tongue meatballs, duck tongue, monkfish liver pâté with miso and a dessert made by Benton herself featuring candied tripe with toasted sesame panna cotta and cardamom crepes. "Not only have I met tons of great people from charities and nonprofits, but I've met a lot of chefs," she said. "And meeting the people has really tied me to the community."

Benton solidified her commitment to the Milwaukee area when she purchased the National Café building in fall 2014. And the decision opened up a whole new world of possibilities. "Owning the building means I can make long-term plans for upkeep, as well as tweaking areas such as the back patio."

Improvements have included a complete remodel of the restaurant's bathroom, as well as new lighting in the dining area. Outdoors, Benton has installed an attractive wooden fence behind the restaurant. She plans to increase the size of the current patio, adding a vegetable and herb garden, as well as flowerbeds scattered throughout the enclosure. She hopes to host a series of summer gatherings there to let people enjoy good food in the open air.

Collaborations

Ask any chef in the Cream City, and they are likely to tell you that one of the best things about the city is its cooperative atmosphere. In Milwaukee, working together goes far beyond the usual collaborative dinners. Culinarians regularly share trade secrets, sources for product and feedback about projects and dishes. They also support one another by eating at area establishments and making local recommendations to diners. In some cases, they partner to open restaurants.

Although the bottom line in the restaurant industry is often slim, most restaurateurs are motivated more by their desire to create than by the drive to secure financial success. However, area collaborations are almost always strategic enterprises forged by shared passion and complementary skill sets. And while they may not meet with immediate financial gratification, these partnerships often ensure the longevity and success of the businesses themselves.

Ross Bachhuber, Melissa Buchholz and Daniel Jacobs, Odd Duck

Ross Bachhuber, chef and co-owner at Odd Duck in Bay View, is the unassuming, quiet type who prefers a place behind the scenes. Co-owner Melissa Buchholz is a front-of-the-house dynamo with a knack for customer service. Executive Chef Daniel Jacobs is has a personality that begs for the

Melissa Buchholz, Ross Bachhuber and Daniel Jacobs of Odd Duck. *Photo by Joe Laedtke.*

spotlight. But the synergy between the three is part of what makes things work at Odd Duck, a spot that's known for its ever-changing menu of inventive and internationally inspired small plates.

Bachhuber, who moved to Milwaukee to earn his degree in art, found his calling in the service industry while working his way through school. Beginning as sous chef for the Astor Hotel, he soon moved on to take executive chef roles at the Milwaukee Art Museum, Lowlands Restaurant Group and Piano Blu on Pewaukee Lake.

Buchholz earned her English degree at University of Wisconsin–Madison, where she spent her free time working as a bartender. She moved to Milwaukee with her now ex-husband, who was attending culinary school at Milwaukee Area Technical College. After working in food and beverage for an area hotel, she signed on to work with the Diablos Rojos group, with whom she opened two restaurants, including Café Centraal.

Buchholz and Bachhuber met at a time when both were looking for a change. "We didn't have any money. Banks wouldn't look at us," said Buchholz. "But we thought, even if we make sub sandwiches, we'd rather do that for ourselves than work for other people."

So, the two gathered up every last cent they could find and made a move. Their first step was to identify a space they could work with. Everything else came second. "We were going to adjust the concept based on the space," said Buchholz. "It wasn't our dream restaurant, but we knew enough about ourselves to know we could create something of quality."

When they found a storefront on the main drag in Bay View that had once housed a small café, they knew they could make it work. "We never really set out to create a small-plates restaurant," noted Bachhuber, "but the kitchen was built, and that's more or less what the space dictated to us."

The two opened Odd Duck in April 2012 with minimal renovation. Bachhuber built tables from pressed sorghum and used cork to line the bar top. Farmstead chairs were painted turquoise to add a colorful pop, while wall-mounted antlers, mason jar lighting and overhead tropical reed fans gave the restaurant a casual flair.

Although Bachhuber has always remained at the helm, under his leadership the kitchen at Odd Duck soon became a creative breeding ground, hosting a cast of characters from around town, including Paul Zerkel and Lisa Kirkpatrick (Roots chefs who would eventually open Goodkind), Shay Linkus (now chef at the Vanguard) and eventually Daniel Jacobs, who was hired as executive chef in 2014.

"It's evolved so much," said Bachhuber, "and the collaboration has been part of that. I believe that people do their best work if you let them do what they love, if they can explore and be creative. So, dishes at the Odd Duck are constantly evolving, and depending on who is in the kitchen, the menu has changed along the way."

These days, Bachhuber divides his time between collaborating with Jacobs in the kitchen and handling other aspects of their booming business. "We all have an insatiable desire to do more and creative things," said Bachhuber. "And I love working off of people in the kitchen."

Jacobs—a Chicago native whose résumé included work at North Pond, Bistro Campagne, Green Zebra, Tru and Naha before he took over the reins at Milwaukee's Roots and Wolf Peach—has contributed his own style to the menu, largely through his love of gadgetry and experimentation. "Dan loves foams, *sous vide*, purees, dehydrators, meat glue, Cryovac machines, centrifuges," said Buchholz. "He will take a good dish and change components to make it more interesting and complex."

Jacobs said that the restaurant is like no other he's seen. "The level of what we do here is incredible," he said. "There's freedom in doing whatever you want. I've never worked a job like it. There are no boundaries. Want to try a new technique? Something weird? Duck hearts, duck balls, it doesn't matter. You just make it taste good."

VAL AND ADAM LUCKS,
HONEYPIE AND PALOMINO BAR

Among Milwaukee's dynamic culinary duos, brother-sister team Adam and Val Lucks might be the best recognized. After all, the two have sustained a successful streak of opening and rehabbing the concepts for some of Milwaukee's most popular cafés and eateries, including Comet, Honeypie and Palomino Bar.

The two started off on opposite ends of the career spectrum. Val had an established career in the corporate world. Meanwhile, Adam pursued his culinary degree at the Le Cordon Bleu–certified Western Culinary Institute in Portland, Oregon. But before Adam graduated, the two started hatching a plan to start their own restaurant. "We were looking at spots in Chicago," Adam recalled, "but Val had a good friend, Scott Johnson, who was here in Milwaukee. We started talking to him and his partner, Leslie [Montemurro], about how to get started, and they were really the ones who persuaded us to make Milwaukee home."

In 2005, the Luckses entered into a partnership with Montemurro and Johnson, taking over the operation of a small coffee shop on Milwaukee's East

Adam and Valerie Lucks of Honeypie Café and Palomino. *Photo by Joe Laedtke.*

Side. "Comet was ten years old," remembered Val, "and the neighborhood had really changed since they'd established it. It needed a refresh. We had the concept for this café—something in the middle—that prepared really good classic, recognizable food with really great ingredients."

At the time, she recalled, Milwaukee had some fine dining restaurants. The city also had a lot of really low-end bar food. But there was not much in between. "We really wanted to fill that gap," Adam added. "We got started in Milwaukee because the opportunity was here. We wanted to do something that was wanted and needed, and Comet turned out to be that thing."

One of the elements the partners felt strongly about was sourcing products locally. So, from the beginning, they made it a point to reach out to local farms. "It was tough at first," recalled Val. "We were turning out such high volume, and at first we couldn't find a place to source enough eggs."

But thanks to a fortuitous connection with Dave Swanson, Comet became one of the first members of the Braise RSA program. "I'll never forget," Adam said. "The first thing we could get in bulk was onions from LoTFoTL. We were going through at least 150 pounds of onions a week, and when Dave told us that [LoTFoTL owner] Tim Huth's field had flooded and that he'd had to pull all of his onions, we agreed to take them. They were so tiny, but we took them and we sat there, peeling them all."

Meanwhile, Comet's reputation grew, and the restaurant became a neighborhood destination for great, high-quality food without all the fuss. "We were making our own stocks, buying good ingredients and using all the same techniques as higher-end restaurants. But we were making mac and cheese, pancakes and sandwiches—things people could eat every day."

As Comet became better established, Val found herself able to leave her corporate career behind, eventually joining Adam in the kitchen, where she led the charge in making the restaurant's baked goods, including pies and biscuits.

As the bakery business grew, the Luckses realized that they'd soon need a new facility to accommodate the demand. So, when their partners began looking at spaces in the Bay View area, it piqued their interest. "We didn't want to open another Comet," Adam noted, "but we saw the space and saw that we could build a bakery kitchen. So we talked about creating a menu that really fit the neighborhood."

The timing was near perfect. The partners had developed increased traction with local sourcing but were still struggling with the overall costs it incurred. "Opening a second restaurant allowed us to increase our volume,

Honeypie Café. *Photo by Joe Laedtke.*

making it more affordable to source the way we wanted to," said Adam. "I also wanted to flex my muscles a bit and start going a little bit more upscale for dinner, so Honeypie allowed me to do that."

It turned out that 2009 was the best and the worst year all at the same time. Just one month after Honeypie Café opened, Comet was featured on the Food Network's *Diners, Drive-Ins and Dives.* "Our volume literally doubled," said Val. "It was a blessing and a curse. It really made us take a long, hard look at the systems we were using to get things done."

In 2013, the Luckses took on their most recent restaurant project, partnering again with Johnson and Montemurro to refresh Palomino Bar, a dive bar and eatery in Bay View. "Palomino was in the same boat that Comet was in at the time," said Val. "The neighborhood had totally changed, and the concept hadn't changed with it. It was something Scott and Leslie loved that they had put a lot of time into, and they didn't want to see it die. But they were focused on other things."

The duo refocused the menu on southern favorites like fried chicken, biscuits and greens, adding touches like house-made hush puppies, jams and desserts. "We're combining the simplicity of Comet's food with the ever-evolving menu of Honeypie," Adam noted. "There's no reason why you can't do bar food with the same philosophy as you can higher-end fare."

Ultimately, the concept of good, simple food is where the Luckses' philosophy begins and ends. "I like fancy food," Val remarked. "But sometimes you just want a fried chicken sandwich. Or a shrimp po-boy, so we have the done-up options for specials, but I like the simplicity. Our shrimp po-boy is just a po-boy. It wasn't made with lasers."

Beginning in 2015, after nearly twelve years of partnership, the Luckses split amiably from their partnership with Scott Johnson and Leslie Montemurro, taking sole ownership of both Honeypie Café and Palomino Bar and giving up their claims to Comet Café. Under the new business name Pie Incorporated, the Luckses aspire to expand their wholesale baking business.

Chris Hatleli and Nick Burki, Coquette Café

For Chefs Nick Burki and Chris Hatleli, March 1, 2010, was a day to be remembered. It was, after all, the day on which mentors Sanford and Angie D'Amato handed over the reigns for Coquette Café, a French bistro in Milwaukee's Third Ward modeled after the D'Amatos' memories of Paris. "After ten years of Sanford being a destination, we wanted to open something where we could see people once a week," said Chef Sanford D'Amato. "And doing a true bistro was something I really wanted to do."

Bartolotta's Lake Park Bistro had opened in 1995, a brasserie-style restaurant with a focus on higher-end cuisine. But D'Amato envisioned something more accessible, with entrées under sixteen dollars and a wine list of selections under twenty dollars. "We wanted to open a bistro-type restaurant like we'd experienced the first time we went to Paris," said D'Amato. "I'll never forget—we'd just had dinner, and we were stuffed. But we were walking down a side street, and there was this glow coming out of a window. The bistro was packed with people. And immediately there was this feeling—I was almost hungry again, and I wanted to be in there. That's what we wanted to create with the new restaurant."

Things fell into place when real estate developer George Bockl approached the D'Amatos with a proposition. He had a building that currently housed a restaurant called the Milwaukee Room, but it was struggling, and Bockl hoped D'Amato could help to transform it into a thriving eatery. "I remember standing outside the restaurant before we opened," D'Amato said, "and the

Coquette Café. *Photo by Joe Laedtke.*

lighting had just been set up. And it had that glow I remembered from Paris. I was almost tearing up; it was exactly what we wanted it to be."

When Coquette Café opened in 1999, the menu included Milwaukee's first hangar steak, as well as coq au vin and French onion soup. And the atmosphere provided a quiet respite from the Milwaukee street—precisely as D'Amato had hoped.

The D'Amatos ran Coquette for ten years before deciding to sell the café in 2009. At that point, Chefs Burki and Hatleli were the natural choice. The two chefs met while working at Sanford in the early 1990s and later became part of the opening crew at Coquette. Hatleli began his career at Sanford as a dishwasher, where his interest in fine dining evolved. By 1992, after meeting Julia Child at the restaurant, his goals had changed. "I asked Sandy if I could cook, and he told me that I needed to go to culinary school," Hatleli recalled.

So, Hatleli enrolled in culinary school at Milwaukee Area Technical College. "My parents had divorced when I was thirteen," said Hatleli, "and Sandy became my mentor. He became a father that you didn't want to disappoint. And for a chef of Sandy's caliber to apprentice an inner-city kid like me, it was amazing. Sandy and Angie gave me the hope of an American dream again."

Burki, on the other hand, had plans to be an actor and musician. So he originally intended to use his culinary career as a fallback plan. "I went to Waukesha Area Technical College," said Burki. "While I was there, [instructor] Louis DeAngelis was the guy who really instilled in me the passion and love for cooking. He always talked about Sanford—that it was one of the best restaurants in the country. So, my dream was to maybe someday work there." When a position opened at Sanford, he jumped on it.

After Burki and Hatleli opened Coquette, they went on to work together, opening the original Social restaurant on South Second Street before parting ways. They were reunited in 2006 as co-chefs at the Milwaukee Art Museum's Café Calatrava, where both were chosen to prepare Valentine's Day dinner at the James Beard House in New York City. "Two Milwaukee boys hit a home run that night," said Hatleli. "It was Fashion Week, and the city was abuzz. The whole experience was very humbling."

The two were humbled again when the D'Amatos approached them to take over Coquette Café. "He wanted to let us take care of his 'baby,'" Hatleli said. "It was a big responsibility. But he knew we were ready."

Burki and Hatleli kept most of the existing staff at the restaurant, and they remained true to Coquette's mission of producing high-quality French cuisine. But the road was rocky starting out. In 2009, the economic downturn hit Milwaukee in full force. "It was a hard time," Hatleli said. "I think people were scared to go out and spend what they had. We were lucky, though. We got good press coming out of the gates. Restaurant critic Carol Deptolla gave us three and a half stars. And that helped."

It also helped to have a loyal following. "It wasn't a weight—the legacy of being a restaurant that Sandy D'Amato started," noted Hatleli. "It just meant that you knew what had to be done."

Burki agreed. "Even today, it means staying true to the concept," he said. "It's all about the food. And we want to re-create the idea that you're in a bistro in Paris. I think that's the thing I like most about the place. You come in here, and you can feel like you're not in Milwaukee for a minute. It's a break from reality."

March 2015 marked five years of the partners' ownership. And, said Hatleli, so much of what made Coquette great in 1999 is still in place. "The soup onions are still being sliced painstakingly by hand. We're still serving 350 plates of coq au vin," he said. "And ultimately, when the going gets tough, it's best to just put your head down and start slicing."

MARC AND MARTA BIANCHINI, CUBANITAS AND INDULGE WINE ROOM

Marc and Marta Bianchini, the husband-and-wife team behind Get Bianchini, have built a legacy in the city of Milwaukee. But that legacy started in New York. "I always knew I wanted to be a chef and restaurant owner," said Marc. "Ever since my first day of work, making desserts and salads at a restaurant called Crooked Hill in Long Island, I knew."

After graduating from high school at age seventeen, he went directly to the Culinary Institute of America to learn the trade. The aspiring chef completed externships at the Locanda del' Angelo in Liguira, Italy, and at the San Domenico restaurants in New York City and Emilia-Romagna, Italy. At San Domenico in New York, he crossed paths with Paul Bartolotta, who invited Bianchini to Milwaukee to help start Ristorante Bartolotta in Wauwatosa.

Once Marc's work at Ristorante was complete, Bianchini next moved on to Lettuce Entertain You Enterprises, the high-profile Chicago restaurant chain. There he explored new markets and foods. By 1994, at age twenty-three, Bianchini had returned to Milwaukee with his wife, Marta, and started Osteria Del Mondo, his first restaurant.

At the time, Milwaukeeans were largely unfamiliar with authentic Italian cuisine. "We weren't serving large portions of pasta. We didn't serve caprese when tomatoes weren't in season," said Marc. "When we brought people an *assaggio*—a little tasting—they asked us why we were bringing them food they didn't order."

Marc and Marta Bianchini of Get Bianchini. *Photo by Joe Laedtke.*

But by May of that year, Marc Bianchini had made the cover of *Milwaukee Magazine*. And his drive pushed him to be the best of the best. "Some nights I had to sleep at the restaurant," he recalled. "The seafood trucks from Chicago came through between 3:00 a.m. and 5:00 a.m., so I would sleep in the vestibule. The trucks would stop by twice a week—every Monday and Thursday night."

And while Osteria worked its way onto yearly lists of "Top 30 Restaurants," the Bianchinis embarked on additional projects. In 2003, they opened the casually hip Cubanitas on Milwaukee Street. The restaurant zeroed in on authentic Cuban fare, including empanadas, *croquetas*, *tostones* and *ropa vieja*, with specials like *boliche*, Cuban-style pot roast with chorizo and rice. "Nine years later, people were quicker to embrace ethnic food," Marta recalled. "Our menu was based on my family's recipes, and there was nothing like it in the city."

In the meantime, Marc took on consulting projects for area restaurants including Kil@watt, Carnevor and Sake Tumi. But by 2008, the Bianchinis were itching to work on another concept of their own, so they opened Indulge Wine Room, an extravagant destination for wine, chocolate, cheese and charcuterie.

"Everything was going well. Osteria was good, Cubanitas was good, consulting was good. And I decided I wanted to give people a real wine bar. It took forever for that to take root," Marc recalled. "But in the end, Indulge forced people to change. It forced other wine bars to improve their cheese selections. And then, all of a sudden, charcuterie plates were popping up everywhere."

In 2012, after a lease fell through for a new location, the Bianchinis made the tough decision to close Osteria. The year it closed, Osteria made the *USA Today*'s list of the top twenty-five restaurants in the country. "I'm still proud of the restaurant," said Marc. "It ruffled a lot of feathers. Not only was I a New Yorker, but I was a twenty-three-year-old New Yorker. But it was one of the best restaurants in Milwaukee, and it forced the city to up its game."

Bianchini said that the restaurant's closing was a blow. But he doesn't view it as an ending. "I'm proud of what we've accomplished," he noted. "We've taken risks. We've pushed. In hindsight, I feel like we should have fought a bit more. But it's still my dream to reopen the restaurant someday. If Osteria comes back, we want to be in a landmark, in the best building, with the best location."

PAUL ZERKEL AND LISA KIRKPATRICK, GOODKIND

Five industry folks, one iconic Milwaukee pizza joint and a collective dream. These are the things of which the Bay View restaurant, Goodkind, is made.

Enter talented chefs Paul Zerkel and Lisa Kirkpatrick. Throw in the ever-energetic lawyer turned prodigious bartender Katie Rose of Burnhearts, along with über-industrious Burnheart's Bar owners Jessica and William (B.J.) Seidel, and you have the deceptively motley—but almost superheroish—crew that took on the job of bringing new life to the tired space at 2457 South Wentworth Avenue, formerly the home of Mama de Marini's, a longtime Italian restaurant dating back to the 1950s that closed in 2012.

The dream was a long time in coming for Chefs Zerkel and Kirkpatrick,

Paul Zerkel and Lisa Kirkpatrick of Goodkind. *Photo by Joe Laedtke.*

who met in the early 1990s and have worked together at a variety of restaurants including Roots in Milwaukee. Zerkel, who was born and bred in Wauwatosa, entered the food industry at a young age, frying up eggrolls for Asian restaurant Wong's Wok at Summerfest when he was thirteen. He moved on to the Chancery, where he was on the first line when it opened, and later left to become kitchen manager at the Shorewood Inn. "I was good at the work, and it paid the bills," said Zerkel. "But I was a musician at heart, and I didn't really have dreams of being a chef."

Nick Burki (now owner of Coquette Café), who was lead singer in Zerkel's band, Soma, introduced him to

Lisa Kirkpatrick, a sous chef who worked with him at Pieces of Eight on the lakefront.

Kirkpatrick, who was from northern Illinois, dropped out of an economics program at Illinois State after realizing that she had no desire to end up chained to a desk for the remainder of her career. She took a job working in the kitchen at a local homeless shelter. And it got her thinking about a culinary career.

When she moved back home to care for her father, who'd sustained injuries in a skiing accident, she worked at a supper club, where she met a colleague who suggested she pursue a culinary degree at Milwaukee Area Technical College. "I'd never really thought about Milwaukee," she confessed, "but the idea stuck."

She started the culinary program there but dropped out to take a full-time position at Pieces of Eight, a lakeside fine dining restaurant that now houses Harbor House, a Bartolotta's Restaurant. When she met Zerkel, she said, things got serious fairly quickly. She told him of aspirations to travel and work on the West Coast, and the two decided to try something new. They packed up their Cadillac Coup de Ville and went on the road, ending up in Portland, Oregon, where they each took positions in restaurant kitchens. "It was the beginning of my chef career," said Zerkel. "Our time in Portland became about me evolving into a chef and Lisa becoming a better one."

Zerkel landed at Gino's, an Italian trattoria. Meanwhile, Kirkpatrick got experience in Spanish and Italian cuisine working at restaurants like Tapeo and Nostrana. Over the course of ten years in Portland, both chefs honed their craft in the kitchen, as well as gained experience abroad—Zerkel in Italy, where he worked in Alba during the truffle festival, and Kirkpatrick in Spain, where she fell in love with the culture and flavors of the local cuisine.

When Kirkpatrick returned from her second trip to Spain, she found Zerkel waiting, engagement ring in hand. When the two married, they honeymooned in Paris, where they fell in love with a bistro that specialized in succulent rotisserie-roasted meats and vegetables cooked beneath the meaty drippings. It was an indelible experience—one to which they'd return once they established Goodkind in 2014.

In 2005, the two returned to Milwaukee, a city they saw building a culinary prowess. "We kept coming back, and every time we could see the city growing," Zerkel said. "You saw the feel of the place. You'd go out to eat and see that people were starting to pay more attention."

Zerkel took a job as sous chef at Roots, where he developed relationships with farmers and perfected the art of leaf-to-root cooking and preserving. "I learned so much from John [Raymond]," he said. "Every piece of vegetable, every part, deserves to be honored. He was very Zen-like that way. And it made an impression."

When Zerkel fell into the position of chef after the departure of Roots' chef de cuisine, he hired Kirkpatrick, who had been working with Chef Kevin Sloan at the Social. She took over the pastry program there, expanding her skillset to include a vast array of desserts. "We collaborated, did dinners and wrote menus together," said Kirkpatrick, "and as we wrote together, we really grew and found our collective style."

Years later, when Kirkpatrick's position was cut due to tight finances, Zerkel decided to leave Roots with her. And the two began to explore starting their own restaurant. In the meantime, they launched a pop-up operation called Butcher, Baker and took jobs at Odd Duck and Hinterland to make ends meet. Along the way, they made friends with future partners Rose and the Seidels. When the Seidels approached them about partnering on a new restaurant, things quickly fell into place. "We all were hard workers," said

Goodkind. *Photo by Joe Laedtke.*

Kirkpatrick, "and we all brought different skills to the table. We also realized that we had to dive in and risk everything to do what we wanted to do."

The intense renovation of the De Marini's space took nearly a year, but Goodkind opened in June 2014 to an enthusiastic local reception. The concept, which pulled in elements from each partner's contributions, was unique and fresh. There was a rotisserie and a collaborative menu filled with seasonal comfort food, a craft cocktail list a mile long and a beer list that could please even the geekiest of beer lovers.

And the menu at Goodkind still reeks of heart. The spicy crab bucatini was born of Kirkpatrick's memories of eating on the beach in Oregon. The fennel pollen chicken is a recipe that she and Zerkel created for the wedding of Justin and Sarah Aprahamian, owners of Sanford. "We aim for cuisine that your grandmother would make," said Zerkel with a smile, "…if she went to cooking school, that is."

Dining as an Economic Driver

When most people think of a dining scene, they are likely to envision a community of restaurants, a city with diverse options for food and drink and probably a few celebrity chefs thrown in for good measure. And they aren't wrong.

But a thriving restaurant industry includes a larger measure of components, including accessibility to quality ingredients; artisan food purveyors that are dedicated to singular perfection in products like bread, chocolate and ice cream; a beverage scene that accommodates the desire for interesting beer, wine and cocktails; a new generation of chefs with fresh ideas who promote innovation and change; and destination restaurants that attract tourists.

Milwaukee features all of these. It also includes other economic drivers—largely entertainment venues—that attract newcomers to the city and provide increasingly provocative reasons for both talent and tourists to return again and again. Among these, two that stand out are the Pabst Theater Group and Potawatomi Hotel & Casino, a venue built on the Potawatomi tribal lands that has seen increasing growth and success in the past decade.

PETER GEBAUER,
POTAWATOMI HOTEL & CASINO

When management of seven dining venues is just part of a day's work, it helps to have a world of experience behind you. Fortunately for Milwaukee, Peter Gebauer, executive chef for Potawatomi Hotel & Casino, is both an avid globetrotter and a consummate professional.

Gebauer started his culinary love affair early. At age fifteen, he entered into a three-year apprenticeship at a boutique hotel in Germany, where he earned certification as a chef. From there, he signed on with Royal Viking Cruise line and spent five years sailing around the world, cooking onboard its luxury cruise ships. His global adventures continued as Gebauer proceeded to take his first sous chef position with Peninsula Hotel Group in Hong Kong before moving on to work in Bahrain for two years. "At that point," he said, "I wanted to go back home to Germany to see how I measured up. So, I returned to school and became a Certified Master Chef."

Chef Peter Gebauer of Potawatomi Hotel & Casino. *Photo by Joe Laedtke.*

Shortly thereafter, Gebauer was appointed executive chef onboard the legendary SS *Norway*, the largest cruise ship in the world at the time. "There were four different restaurants on board the ship for guests," he recalled, "Plus eight for crew members. It was a big job."

In the 1990s, Gebauer added work with Disney World Orlando and Disney Cruise Line to his résumé, along with taking on the challenge of assisting with the startup of Star Cruises in Singapore. From there, he moved on to open the Aventura Spa Palace in Cancun and work for the Gaylord Opryland Resort in Nashville, Tennessee.

In 2006, Gebauer accepted the position as executive chef at Potawatomi Bingo Casino. Among his goals for the casino was to create exceptional, unique, world-class dining options. But first he needed to get back to the basics. "At the time," Gebauer noted, "the company had just approved plans for expansion. So, when I arrived, the first thing I had to do was to assess our talent and resources because I knew that in eighteen months we would triple in size."

Gebauer evaluated and reclassified staff and then implemented a training program based on the standards of the Culinary Institute of America. Today, the program features four different levels comprising thirty-one classes taught by Gebauer and other senior chefs.

His second mission was to begin to reeducate the casino's guests. While Dream Dance had established a reputation for fine dining and achieved the AAA Four Diamond Award under the leadership of Chef Jason Gorman, the casino lacked quality in other areas. "It was challenging," Gebauer admitted. "We had to listen to what people wanted—which at the time was cheap food and lots of it. It was slow to bring people around."

But little by little, Gebauer implemented changes. The casino buffet was revamped, the Fire Pit Sports Bar and Grill was added and in 2008 the casino added Ru Yi, a pan-Asian restaurant, and Wild Earth, a contemporary American restaurant offering dishes with seasonal and local ingredients. Ru Yi survived the recession and business grew, but the concept for Wild Earth was discontinued despite early success in food quality and service. So, Gebauer and the team stepped back to square one, revamping the concept and reintroducing it as Wild Earth Cucina, a restaurant with a rustic Italian theme, in 2012.

In 2014, Gebauer also led his team through the Potawatomi Hotel expansion, which included a new restaurant venue, Locavore, with a menu focused on local, seasonal, sustainable fare with global influences.

Gebauer noted that his education in creating seasonal, locally based menus began in Cancun, where he refocused the resort's menu on regional Mexican fare. It continued with his work in Nashville, where regional products, such as local freshwater shrimp and organic stone-ground grits, became staples on the Opryland menu. For most, eating locally is about freshness and quality. But at Potawatomi Hotel Casino, he said, the initiative is as much about the environment as it is about flavor. "These days," Gebauer said, "local sourcing has become mainstream. But it remains our responsibility to really make it work. We have to look at future generations—how are they going to grow up? How will we educate them?"

The concept of leaving as little impact as possible on the environment has been part of the Potawatomi tribe's beliefs and culture for centuries, so Gebauer said that an environmental focus to dining is always front of mind at the casino.

Gebauer has taken local a step further by reclaiming local and regional ingredients like shagbark syrup, papaw and choke cherries, as well as invasive species like Asian carp and snakehead fish, incorporating them into the menus at the casino's restaurants.

He has also been at the helm of waste initiatives, such as the installation of a casino-wide compost digester, which processes between five and eight tons of organic waste each week, offsetting the energy consumption of the casino and hotel. This year, Potawatomi also installed 1,144 solar panels across the property. "Despite everything we're doing," noted Gebauer, "We can always do more."

In the spring of 2015, after nearly a decade with the casino, Gebauer accepted a position as executive chef with Sendik's Food Markets, a family-owned Milwaukee grocer. Gebauer brings more than forty years of culinary expertise to the role, which will include development of additional Sendik's signature recipes, coaching chefs in each of Sendik's twelve kitchens and finding innovative ways to meet consumer needs with products like Sendik's Fresh2GO, a line of prepared food products.

KEVIN SLOAN, PABST THEATER GROUP

Kevin Sloan is known around Milwaukee as the "chef to the stars." His role as chef for Pabst Theater Group means he spends his days and nights preparing meals for the musicians and other entertainers who perform at the Riverside Theater, Pabst Theater and Turner Hall Ballroom. In the past five years, Sloan has cooked meals for Norah Jones, Neil Young, Bon Iver, Jerry Seinfeld, Kevin Hart and countless other celebrities.

Sloan's job is an important one. His work feeds into the success of Milwaukee's ever-growing cultural scene and drives the economic progress that comes with being a city that's attractive to performers around the globe. It's also a chance to showcase the city and everything it has to offer. Sloan often uses local ingredients from his garden (as well as those of his staff), the city's urban farmers' markets and the many cheeses and meats produced in Wisconsin.

"The end goal is to give the performers a great experience in Milwaukee," said Sloan. "There are very few theaters who have their own kitchens and their own chefs. And our business model is really designed to go above and beyond. It's not strictly about the bottom line. It's more about creating an overall experience and ensuring that performers want to come back again and again."

Sloan's menus offer everything from French bistro fare to midwestern classics to Middle Eastern and Asian dishes, all executed with a deft touch. He credits extensive travel, along with experience working with a multitude of talented chefs, with providing the inspiration

Kevin Sloan of the Pabst Theater Group. *Photo by Joe Laedtke.*

for his often globally inspired fare. "Ultimately, I want to be able to make what's needed to have the artists be happy according to their tastes, and my background allows me to do so," Sloan said.

Potentially the most impressive aspect of Sloan's work is that he does it all in a modest kitchen on the eighth floor of the Riverside Theater. The six-burner stove, two ovens and petite hibachi grills provide everything Sloan and his staff need to take care of the world-class artists who perform at the theaters.

But Sloan's legacy in Milwaukee did not begin with the preparation of celebrity dinners. In fact, he played a large role in the early development of Milwaukee's now-thriving restaurant scene. Sloan was born and raised on the northwest side of Milwaukee, where his love for the kitchen began under the tutelage of his mother, Ursula, a first-generation German immigrant. But his culinary career took flight in New Mexico, where he attended culinary school in his early twenties. There he worked at restaurants like the Monte Vista Fire Station, where he learned how to perform on a busy line under Chef Jerry Waquie, who grew up on the Jemez Indian reservation in the mountains of New Mexico. Through his friendship with Waquie, Sloan found himself privy to Native American dances, cooking and culture—elements that escape the experience of many. After his time at Monte Vista, he spent three years cooking in the foothills of Sante Fe at an avante garde, scratch restaurant, where he learned how to make bread and pasta and butcher meats and fish, as well as how to start, maintain and use a garden. Before leaving New Mexico, a friend asked to assist in opening an Asian noodle house in the heart of the city. That experience is where his affinity with Asian ingredients began.

In the mid-1990s, Sloan returned to Milwaukee, where he cooked with Mark Weber at Lake Park Bistro and Sanford D'Amato and Dave Swanson at Sanford. "We did Beard dinners at Sanford where Mario [Batali] would come do a course, along with Terence Brennan and Rocco Dispirito," recalled Sloan. "And through that work and travel, I developed a lot of great connections."

Sloan contemplated leaving Milwaukee to work on the coast but ultimately changed his tune. A conversation with Richard Regner, owner of Soup Brothers in Milwaukee's Walker's Point Neighborhood, inspired him to stay in the city. "At the time, they weren't doing much business there," said Sloan. "But it was a cool little spot. Richard was like, 'Come and hang out. We'll make soup, and we'll rule the world,' and so that's what I did."

Sloan invested in new equipment for the restaurant, including new stoves and a mixer and proofer so that they could make their own bread. And by the time he left the restaurant about a year later, business had quadrupled.

Meanwhile, Sloan started scouting out spots to open his own restaurant. "At the time, there was nothing going on in Milwaukee," he recalled. "There was nothing with a younger vibe, nothing funky. And I thought, 'This is a big city. It can't just have these restaurants that are super high end; we need something different here.'"

When he located a space on South Second Street in Walker's Point, formerly the home of a bar and café called the Filter Inn, he partnered with Bill Deuberry, Nick Burki and Chris Hatleli to open the Social.

It was October 2001. The name of the restaurant was inspired by the name of a Chemical Brothers album, *Live at the Social*, recorded at an underground club in London. In kind, the vibe inside was relaxed and hip and nothing like any other spot in the city. There was almost always a DJ spinning during dinner, and budding bands such as Def Harmonic, Recycled Future and Rusty P's often replaced the tables in the front of the space later in the evening. With an open kitchen behind the bar and a dedicated staff, the Social's menu endeared itself to Milwaukeeans and visitors alike.

Higher-end items like foie gras and sweetbreads sat comfortably alongside white mushroom and butternut squash risotto, warm duck salad with cherries and roasted beets and a notorious mac and cheese prepared with goat cheese, roasted chicken and rosemary, creating options that appealed to a diverse array of palates and pocketbooks.

Business got off to a slow start, but after a positive review in a local paper, the *Shepherd Express*, just before the New Year, the Social became Milwaukee's new hot spot, regularly filling its nearly forty seats with eager customers. "I think we were down to our last $100 when we finally got reviewed, and the word got out that we existed," recalled Sloan. "Without the *Shepherd* article, we may not have lasted another week."

Despite the neighborhood's relative lack of other attractions, the Social began to entice a regular crowd of eager diners and music lovers. "It was fun to see Walker's Point—which was just a lot of beautiful but empty brick warehouses—start to combine with the human element. After a few months, the block was packed, filling up with expensive cars. It was a little shocking to me to be honest. I wasn't sure if we could pull it off… getting people down here."

In 2003, Sloan opened a second restaurant with partner Carrie Torres. Sol Fire was a small restaurant located on Farwell Avenue that served up Latin American–inspired fare like *ropas viejas*, caramelized plantains, jerk chicken, fish tacos and *moqueca*, a Brazilian seafood stew. Although the restaurant filled a niche for Milwaukeeans—and also became a popular spot—failed lease negotiations resulted in its closing in 2007.

Meanwhile, after four years of success at the Social, other restaurants with similar concepts began opening with frequency throughout the metro area. Partners Deuberry, Hatleli and Burki had since moved on, and Sloan sensed that he was losing the traction he once had at the restaurant. This, combined with feeling isolated in the still underdeveloped Walker's Point neighborhood, resulted in a decision to move the restaurant to a new location, an up-and-coming spot at the corner of South First Street and Pittsburgh.

The new Social opened in 2005, but despite a roomier interior in which Sloan tried to re-create the restaurant's former underground vibe, it never took off in the same way that the original location had. When the economy took a major hit at the end of 2008, Sloan ran low on funds and energy. By the following New Year, the Social was closed.

After a few weeks of traveling with his friend and former partner, Torres, who was now living in Barcelona, Sloan worked for a time as the culinary director for the Diablos Rojos group under Mike Eitel. Although the position turned out to be a less than ideal fit, Eitel became the catalyst by which Sloan connected with Gary Witt, head of the Pabst Theater Group. And the rest, as they say, is history.

Looking Forward

When President Obama built his 2012 presidential campaign around the theme "Forward," he could have been talking about the Milwaukee food scene. In 2014, the city saw more than fifty restaurant openings. In the last ten years, it has also seen a sea change in consumer palates and the desire for diversity in cuisines.

Consumer palates across the United States have grown more adventurous and sophisticated, thanks to numerous factors. Starting in 1993, popular television shows like *Top Chef*, *Iron Chef America* and *Hell's Kitchen* began to offer viewers a rare inside look at the culinary industry and provide them with added information on the ingredients and techniques used to prepare their favorite foods. By 2000, Anthony Bourdain's best-selling *Kitchen Confidential* was offering food lovers a knives-out, behind-the-scenes view of life in the culinary fast lane. Add that to an increase in diners sharing their experiences on social media, food blogs and sites like Urban Spoon and Yelp, and you start to see why food is at the top of mind for millions of Americans.

According to a 2012 Culinary Visions Panel survey, 54 percent of casual diners in the United States are labeled as "foodies" and characterized by their desire to try new menu items when visiting restaurant. These adventurous diners are significantly more likely than the general population to choose menu items with bitter, sour and umami flavors. The same survey revealed that 53 percent of U.S. adults regularly watch cooking shows and that 76 percent enjoy talking about new or interesting foods.

And Milwaukeeans are no different. Even in a town once known for basics like beer, bratwurst and Friday fish fries, the desire to try new foods and connect with the chefs preparing their cuisine has incited an increasing interest in restaurants and contributed to growth in the scene.

National coverage by media, including the Travel Channel, the *New York Times*, the *Chicago Tribune* and *Fodor's*, as well as by magazines like *Food & Wine* and *Bon Appétit*, have only fed the frenzy. And Milwaukee has seen an influx of diners traveling up from Chicago to visit Milwaukee restaurants. "Milwaukee has changed a lot," said Joe Muench of Black Shoe Hospitality. "Property is affordable. Owning restaurants is cool, and you can get funding. People also want to eat out a lot more. They want really good experiences with socialization. Ending your day at a restaurant is becoming the norm rather than ending it at home. You may have gone to a bar before, but now you're going to a restaurant, without breaking the bank."

Recent openings have begun to bring more focused concepts to the fore. The Vanguard on Kinnickinnic in Bay View, for instance, specializes in creatively conceived sausages—like chicken with Coca-Cola mole, chicharones, salsa and queso fresco—paired with tap craft cocktails and sides like poutine and baked potato balls.

Morel on South Second Street in Walker's Point has brought new life to locally focused fare, offering a constantly changing selection of mid- to high-end cuisine with global flavors. Dishes like short ribs with silk beans, kimchi and pac choi and ricotta cavatelli made with flour from Wisconsin's Lonesome Stone Milling round out a menu that includes appetizers, salads and a selection of inspired desserts.

And additional openings for 2015 will include Amilinda, a former pop-up shop headed up by Chef Gregory Leon and partner Orry Leon focused on dishes influenced by the flavors of Spain, Portugal and the southern United States; there are plans to settle into a spot on Wisconsin Avenue before the summer has passed. Company Brewing, a brewpub concept launched by former Colectivo Coffee director George Bregar, has taken over a space in Riverwest formerly occupied by Stonefly Brewing Company.

But how long can a city sustain such exponential growth? And where do we go from here? Chefs and restaurateurs have differing opinions.

"What really strikes me about the question of sustainability," said Paul Zerkel of Goodkind, "is that a major point in the growth of Milwaukee was the Pabst Riverside and growth in the entertainment arena. There was a time when no musicians stopped in Milwaukee. You had to go to Chicago, Minneapolis. The resurrection of those theaters began what I hope to be a resurrection of downtown. And restaurants are kind of like flowers that are built on a root system that is downtown. If you make somewhere a destination, people will go there and people eat when they're there."

Jarvis Williams, executive chef at Carnevor, expressed a similar hopefulness. "Chefs of my generation are getting very ambitious in opening up small, quaint shops that are not trying to do large amounts of people but rather cater to a neighborhood while representing themselves through food. It takes time to become a premier destination, but at this rate, Milwaukee will soon be right there with the bigger cities across the country."

But despite an overall sense of optimism about the growing scene, many also speculate that hot spots like Walker's Point and Bay View, which have exploded with new restaurants in recent years, will see some closings in years to come. "It's going to depend upon how the future plays out for the places that have opened and that are opening," said Leslie Montemurro of Mojofuco. "The public will ultimately tell us when we have too many farm-to-table restaurants or macaroni and cheese places or burger joints. And we'll have to respond."

Muench agreed. "There are only so many dollars in this market, so the number of restaurants we have here—it's not sustainable," he said. "The hours of work, the reinvestments into the business and the fact that there's such a slim bottom line—it's going to be challenging in the years ahead."

Restaurateurs speculate that a key to a more sustainable market may be a change in the way restaurant owners look at the concepts they're bringing to the table. Many suggest that expanded options for late-night dining is an obvious area for growth. "If we want to move into the major city scene, the late-night dining has to be more interesting than gyros and pizza," said Daniel Jacobs of Odd Duck.

Restaurants like Goodkind and the Vanguard have placed an emphasis on late-night dining. Boone & Crockett has added a food trailer to its bar, which caters to guests from 4:00 p.m. to 1:00 a.m. And Red Light Ramen, a pop-up ramen shop concept run by Chef Justin Carlisle of Ardent on Friday and Saturday evenings, has given the late-night crowd another dining option. But the culture in Milwaukee has yet to fully embrace what's available. "People's habits have to change to support the late-night scene," said Lisa Kirkpatrick of Goodkind. "People need to put their money where they say they want it and grow accustomed to the fact that it exists."

On the other hand, neighborhood-focused restaurants may be the way of the future, with potential growth in areas that haven't yet seen a multiplicity of restaurants enter their boundaries. "I'd like to see more in Bronzeville, Riverwest and Brewer's Hill," said Montemurro. "Even the areas surrounding Downer and University of Wisconsin–Milwaukee are hungry for growth. There's been so much movement to the Fifth Ward and Bay View, and I suspect that will slow down."

"Walker's Point is going to be a spot where I think we'll see a lot of fluctuation," she continued, "especially since it's more of a destination and doesn't have the population density to support everything that's sprung up there."

Kevin Sloan of the Pabst Theater Group said that he'd really like to see more development in the underserved portions of the city. Although he said he's finished with running restaurants, he noted that the one thing that might bring him out of retirement would be a place that really had possibility to change the city. "If there's one thing that would motivate me to do it all again, it would be the potential for building a connection between the downtown elite and the rest of the city," Sloan said. "I would try to find a place on Fond du Lac Avenue or East North Avenue and make awesome food. Try to bring the community together, you know? Because right now there's no one in those areas making it into any food magazines."

Both Melissa Buchholz and Ross Bachhuber of Odd Duck see potential in the development of more focused concepts around the city. "Everybody can't go and be the next best thing," said Buchholz. "We need to look for niches and holes and needs in the market. I think we'll see a lot more low-key, interesting spots. Ethnic restaurants including Japanese, high-end Indian, Korean BBQ, great Chinese…"

Small plates, a trend that swept into the city—and has persisted and expanded for the past five years—is likely on the way out, chefs predict. But other trends are up-and-coming. "Menu-less dining," said Jacobs. "Places like Ardent are moving in that direction—with a focus on tasting menus—and I'd like to see more of that. I would like people to allow the chef to be more in control of what they're eating."

"I think another trend that will emerge is a resurgence of fine dining," said Chef Adam Lucks. "Hipstery steakhouses, more traditional fine dining. Because people are paying more attention to the food on their plates."

And the emphasis on local food will go beyond commonplace, stretching boundaries with regard to the relationships between individual farmers and restaurants. "Chefs like Justin Carlisle [of Ardent] don't label themselves as farm-to-table," said Cole Ersel of Wolf Peach. "But is he buying his dad's beef? Yes. Buying local milk and produce every week? Yes. Getting foragers in? Yes. Everyone is doing farm-to-table because that's what they should be doing. And that's where the market will continue to expand."

Carlisle agreed. "For me, farm-to-table is about cutting out the middle man and really support the farmers. Let's offer to buy a farmer's entire crop of onions. Let's give them a market. Until that changes more largely, and chefs really seek out those connections, our individuality as restaurants—and our health as a scene—won't develop."

Dan Van Rite of Hinterland Erie Street Gastropub brought it home. "We need to support more local farms," he said. "Everyone just needs to get on the same page and make good food."

Collaboration between chefs—which has become a hallmark of Milwaukee eateries—is also seen as a strength that will continue to allow the market to thrive. "A high tide raises all ships," said Thomas Hauck of c. 1880. "Working together and supporting each other means we all have a better chance at survival."

Val Lucks echoed a similar sentiment. "We all support one another's restaurants," she said. "It's a very collaborative city. In that way, Milwaukee is so different from larger cities just because of the small-town nature."

Of course, the best advice for future restaurateurs looking for success in Milwaukee may well come from legendary Grenadier's chef Knut Apitz, who maintains that service is the heart of a great restaurant—something that has suffered greatly over the years. "Look in the mirror every morning," he said. "Ask yourself, 'Am I doing the best I can?' Good enough is never good enough. But if you know that your job is to make everyone as happy as you possibly can, it's a breeze."

References Consulted

In addition to the sources here, the author relied on in-person, telephone and e-mail interviews with restaurant owners and individuals profiled throughout the book.

Culinary Visions Panel Survey. Chicago, Illinois, 2012. http://culinaryvisions.org/trends/?m=201204.

Gurda, John. *The Making of Milwaukee*. Milwaukee, WI: Milwaukee County Historical Society, 1999.

Holmes, David B., and Wenbin Yuan. *Chinese Milwaukee*. Mount Pleasant, SC: Arcadia Publishing, 2008.

Kennedy, Nancy. *Ford Times Cookbook*. New York: Simon & Schuster, 1968.

Kincaid, Dorothy. "You Favor Regional Recipes and Ethnic Meals: Gourmet Admires Restaurants in Milwaukee." *Milwaukee Sentinel*, March 31, 1977. http://news.google.com/newspapers?nid=1368&dat=19770331&id=InpQAAAAIBAJ&sjid=3BEEAAAAIBAJ&pg=7224,646383.

Kubley, Herbert. "Dining Out with Herbert Kubley: Eugene's." *Milwaukee Journal*, May 9, 1971. https://news.google.com/newspapers?id=JfojAAAAIBAJ&sjid=mxAEAAAAIBAJ&pg=895%2C2348647.

Langson, William J. *Thirtieth Annual Report of the Trade and Commerce of Milwaukee*. Milwaukee, WI: King, Fowle & Company, 1888. https://books.google.com/books?id=Cj82AQAAMAAJ&pg=PA1#v=onepage&q&f=false.

Masters, Carol. *Dining In—Milwaukee: A Collection of Gourmet Recipes for Complete Meals from Milwaukee's Finest Restaurants*. Seattle, WA: Peanut Butter Pub, 1981.

Milwaukee Sentinel. "Milwaukee Famed for Good Food." July 4, 1963. https://news.google.com/newspapers?id=JfojAAAAIBAJ&sjid=mxAEAAAAIBAJ&pg=895%2C2348647.

Olesen, Don. "Blind Gourmet Tastes the Food that Makes Milwaukee Famous." *Milwaukee Journal*, April 19 1970. https://news.google.com/newspapers?id=jnUfAAAAIBAJ&sjid=RSgEAAAAIBAJ&pg=4376%2C5835949.

Parnell, Dorothy. "Well Done Frenchy! Rare Honor for Steak." *Milwaukee Sentinel*, June 9, 1951. https://news.google.com/newspapers?id=xXIxAAAAIBAJ&sjid=RRAEAAAAIBAJ&pg=7067%2C55930.

Rothenbueler Maher, Jill. "Branko Radicevic—Restaurateur Knows Hardship, Brings Smiles." *Bay View Compass*, April 1, 2010. http://bayviewcompass.com/branko-radicevic%E2%80%94restaurateur-knows-hardship-brings-smiles/#sthash.verG3ymV.dpuf.

Rowlands, Clarice. "Grace, Charm Exemplify Tea Room." *Milwaukee Journal*, August 5, 1965. http://news.google.com/newspapers?nid=1499&dat=19650805&id=ywYjAAAAIBAJ&sjid=rScEAAAAIBAJ&pg=5340,2864692.

Sherman, Roger, Ron Snyder and Larry Tarnoff. "Milwaukee's Best Bars of Yesteryear, Part Two." OnMilwaukee.com, June 8, 2006. http://onmilwaukee.com/bars/articles/yesteryearbars2.html.

United States Department of Agriculture. "Census of Agriculture." 2012. http://www.agcensus.usda.gov/Publications/2012.

Whitaker, Jan. Restaurant-ing Through History. http://restaurant-ingthroughhistory.com.

———. *Tea at the Blue Lantern Inn: A Social History of the Tea Room Craze in America.* New York: St. Martin's Press, 2002.

Wisconsin Department of Agriculture, Trade and Consumer Protection. "Wisconsin Agriculture by the Numbers." 2014. http://datcp.wi.gov/Newsroom/Facts_and_Figures.

Index

INDEX

INDEX

INDEX

About the Author

A self-proclaimed eater, writer and storyteller, LORI FREDRICH's universe is fashioned of the magic that happens when food meets words. Born and raised in the Milwaukee area, she has tried to leave many times but seems to be drawn to the quirky city that smells of beer and alewives.

As dining writer for Milwaukee's online city magazine, OnMilwaukee. com, Lori aims to bring a fresh perspective to the burgeoning culinary scene, shedding light on the talent in the Milwaukee metro area and using the power of food to build bridges and promote a sense of community in the city.

Photo by Paul Sloth.

Lori's recipes and writing have also been featured in *GO: Airtran Inflight Magazine*, *Cooking Light* magazine, *Edible Milwaukee* and the *Milwaukee Journal Sentinel*, as well as on the blog "Go Bold with Butter," the website Wisconsin Cheese Talk and in the quarterly online magazine *Grate. Pair. Share.*

About the Photographer

J OE LAEDTKE is a professional photographer and food enthusiast born and raised in Milwaukee. His photography has appeared in many local and national publications and been featured on *CBS National News*. He is currently the art director for *Edible Milwaukee* magazine, and when he's not out documenting the city's food scene and residents, he's listening to his ever-multiplying vinyl LP collection or honing his craft at Cantonese cooking. He lives with his manic Tuxedo cat, Theo, on Milwaukee's West Side.

Photo by Jen Ede.

Visit us at
www.historypress.net
....
This title is also available as an e-book